An amalgamation of

Pre-Therapy and Person-Centred Counselling

Reaching the Distant Client

Bernadette Smith

ACKNOWLEDGEMENTS

To Steve, though you are not here to see it, I know you would be proud.

To Martin because I love you.

To my friends and therapists

Anne Cohen, Denton French, John McKenzie, Julie Moorby, Andrew Webb.

Through your support, encouragement and patience, I got to where I am.

To everybody not mentioned, I express my gratitude.

TABLE OF CONTENTS

INTRODUCTION

This book is a continuum of experience from Pre-Therapy material already published and being used. What I aim to give the reader is an insight into how this material is relevant to everyday practice, and the encouragement to 'give it a go'.

Pre-Therapy was developed as a means of working with severely contact impaired clients who were unable to communicate on a normal level of functioning due to their complex disabilities. From this, Van Werde integrated Pre-Therapy into what he terms as 'grey zone contact', where the psychotic client may at times be better functioning, and so he weaves his way between Pre-Therapy reflections and person-centred therapy.

The way in which I use Pre-Therapy is further down the line with clients who would be classed as normal functioning but who may have pre-expressive experiences. Therefore. I use more person-centred therapy, with Pre-Therapy woven through it.

In everyday practice, where clients refer themselves for counselling, it is not to say that they do not have mental health difficulties, learning difficulties or mental illness. There is a range of symptoms associated with mental illness, which present in varying degrees of severity. Each illness presents differently in each person and so the treatment for each person is different too.

Mental illness may refer to permanent or temporary difficulties based on ability in conceptual, social or practical skills caused by genetics, trauma or environment, and could present as psychosis, hallucinations, depression, social withdrawal, delusions, nervousness, anxiety, phobias, and so on.

In some cases, a sufferer may never have disclosed their symptoms but may experience communication difficulties, severe distress or suffer from a psychotic episode without anybody else knowing. They may have never spoken about these for fear of being labelled or do not know how to describe their symptoms. Equally, they may not realise that they have symptoms because, to the person involved, the experience may just seem 'normal'.

During therapy, these hidden symptoms of distress may appear, and it is at that point that Pre-Therapy becomes a tool in the therapist's basket.

CHAPTER 1:

THE DEVELOPMENT OF PRE-THERAPY AND THE DIFFERENCE TO TRADIONAL PERSON-CENTRED COUNSELLING

Carl Rogers developed Person/Client-centred therapy and gave us 'Six therapeutic conditions for growth and change'. He called his therapy 'a therapist construct'; meaning the attitude of the therapist to follow the client's lead and to communicate unconditional positive regard, empathy and congruence in a completely non-directive way. "Experiencing, for the client is therefore a result of the therapy" (Prouty, Van Werde, Portner, 1994).

Eugene Gendlin studied under Rogers and added a new development to person-centred therapy called 'Focusing'. He called this 'a client construct'. Gendlin uses his style of working "to direct the client to their experience, where they learn to facilitate the experiencing process." "Experiencing is a cause of therapy, it is essential to therapeutic change." (Prouty, Van Werde, Portner, 1994)

Gendlin and Rogers worked together at a hospital in Wisconsin on a range of material, with patients suffering from schizophrenia. The results of their study showed a lack of significant movement between the tested and the control groups. From this, Rogers stated, "Retarded clients lack the autonomy and introspective skills required for Client Centred Therapy." In agreement, Gendlin (1970) stated, "It is not so much what is there, as what is not there";

3

meaning the clients' inability to communicate their experience or to make contact with the therapist.

Bearing all of this in mind, the general outcome seemed to be that the control group of clients suffering from schizophrenia were contact impaired, out of contact and unable to make contact with the therapist; thereby preventing productive therapy. Rogers and Gendlin held the clients' inability to communicate responsible for the lack of significant movement and, sadly, at this point they became divided in their work.

Interestingly, Gendlin only recognised the differences between himself and Rogers' work after reading Prouty's first graduate paper, 'The different nature of experiencing between Gendlin and Rogers'; meaning the 'therapist construct' and the 'client construct', to which Prouty remembers him saying, "So that's how we are different." Rogers initially turned down the opportunity to look at Prouty's work during the 1970s, stating that he did not work with such a client group as people suffering from psychosis or learning disabilities. It was in 1986 that Rogers finally listened to Prouty speaking on Pre-Therapy, to which he commented on its significant movement in the Person-Centred approach.

He furthered his study and looked closely at the outcome of the Wisconsin project and the reason attributed to the lack of significant movement, whereby he suggested that Rogers' theory of the therapeutic conditions which influenced both practitioners may itself have been an obstruction and may have limited the process.

Exploration of the foundations on which Prouty based his theory begins by looking at Rogers six hypothesised 'necessary conditions for a therapeutic relationship'. Rogers suggested that these conditions, when adhered to by the therapist, would "offer to the client the best situations for growth and empowerment" (Rogers, 1951). These therapeutic conditions are:

1. Two persons are in Psychological Contact.
2. The first person, whom we shall term 'the client', is in a state of incongruence, being vulnerable or anxious.
3. The second person, whom we shall term 'the therapist', is congruent or is integrated in the relationship.
4. The therapist experiences unconditional positive regard for the client.
5. The therapist experiences an empathic understanding of the client's internal frame of reference and endeavours to communicate this experience to the client.
6. The communication to the client of the therapist's empathic understanding and unconditional positive regard is, to a minimal degree, achieved.

There are three core conditions out of the six with which the person-centred counsellor works. They are Conditions, 3, 4 and 5.

Condition 3

Congruence, 'a way of being'. "Congruence is the state of being of the counsellor, when her outward responses to her client consistently match the inner feelings and sensations which she has in relation to the client." (Mearns & Thorne, 1999). The implicit and explicit communications of what the client has said and the underlying felt sense of self as therapist.

Condition 4

'An attitude' of unconditional positive regard. The therapist makes no judgements either toward the client nor the content of what the client says. Offering only positive regard, unconditionally, to the client, who has previously only received positive regard when adhering to the conditions of worth, will create space for the individual client to get in touch with their true self. Making way for congruence and the unloading of conditions of worth, therefore "Creating a climate of change and growth" (Mearns & Thorne, 1999).

Condition 5

Empathy. 'A process' of walking "as if" (Rogers, 1980) in the client's shoes. "The 'as if' quality of empathy is a crucial aspect of the professionalism of the person-centred counsellor" (Mearns, 1999). It is not the client she perceives, but the client's perception that she shares. "Client and counsellor both become the perceiver, and the client's world becomes the perceived" (Brazier, 1993).

There are two conditions out of the six which refer to the client. They are Conditions 2 and 6.

Condition 2

Refers to the client's state of mind. It is usual for the clients seeking therapy to be in a state of incongruence. A general feeling that something somewhere just isn't right. It may be one or more of many feelings, anxiety, depression, grief, etc.

Condition 6

This depends on whether or not the client is able to receive or acknowledge the empathy being offered. The counsellor can only endeavour to communicate this understanding for the process to be therapeutic and to benefit the therapeutic process; empathy does have to be received.

The remaining condition refers to both the client and the counsellor.
Condition 1
"Two persons are in Psychological Contact." Rogers gives no clear explanation of what this means or how it is achieved, although he does refer to being in Psychological Contact in his writings.

From applying and exploring Prouty's suggestion relating to the limitations of Rogers' hypothesised therapeutic conditions within the Wisconsin project, it is found that:

- Condition 1, that two people are in Psychological Contact", was missing. The clients and therapists at Wisconsin were not in Psychological Contact. In fact, there was little communicative contact of any kind.
- Condition 5, that the therapist experiences an empathic understanding of the client's internal frame of reference and endeavours to communicate this experience to the client, was also missing. The therapist could not understand the client's internal frame of reference and so could not empathise, thereby limiting the therapist.
- Condition 6, that the client receives the unconditional positive regard or empathy that the therapist would offer, was also missing

because the client could not receive this even though the therapist would strive to hold and offer that value.

- From Rogers' non-directive way of working, the therapist follows the client's lead, but the therapists were unable to see any lead from the client, so this did not happen.

- From Gendlin's perspective, the therapist needs to engage with the client in order to lead the client to get in touch with their experiences. This was also missing because there was no engagement between the therapist and the client.

- It may also be that the clients in the Wisconsin project were not in a state of incongruence. The patients may have been hospitalised because the doctors and therapists diagnosed them as mentally ill with some incongruences. If the client did not recognise their own incongruence there would be no Condition 2 either.

From these findings, Prouty continued his work. Gendlin observed that Prouty was obtaining results in areas where he and Rogers were not and, eventually, it was realised that Prouty was picking up where the two models – Pure Person-Centred and Focusing – individually had failed. Prouty, successfully amalgamated their similarities and differences, because "they present a working paradigm."

Certainly, a major part of Prouty's new development and interest in enabling contact came about due to his experience and painful memories of Bobby, his brother, who suffered with mental illness. Prouty recalls heart-breaking memories of Bobby's loneliness and isolation, of him rocking back and forth, holding his head in his hands, unable to make contact with those around him, and singing over and over again, "My heart cries for you, sighs for you." With hindsight, Prouty felt that this was probably Bobby's way of expressing the abandonment that he was experiencing when he sat alone for hours. He tells us, "I know I carried empathic pain for his isolation. My regret to this day is that I did not play with him and give him more loving attention" (Prouty, 2002).

Like Rogers, Prouty had grown up in a dysfunctional family situation, and his writing talks of his experience of "physical cruelty and contemptuous dismissal of his thoughts and feelings." He was a gifted child but this was overlooked, regardless of the fact that a psychiatrist had spoken to his parents about it. The effect of his neglectful and violent upbringing left him feeling worthless and affected his life for many years. When Gendlin complimented him on his work many years later, Prouty failed to see his own value and thought that Gendlin was just being kind. The full awareness of his own giftedness came to light after watching a film about such children, where "self-recognition sent me out of the classroom crying" (Prouty, 2002). Prouty received the highest score that the college had seen in 25 years.

It is as a result of this background and understanding of poverty, neglect and abuse, the deep empathy that he felt for his brother, along with his understanding of person-centred and experiential therapy that Prouty came to develop Pre-Therapy.

Therapeutic Process of Pre-Therapy

- Client is unaware of anyone, including the counsellor, and is in their own reality.
- Therapist strives to make empathic contact.
- Is directed by the therapist in that it aims to facilitate development of the client's capacity for contact; an awareness of self and others.
- Therapist's understanding of the client's world is not important.
- Therapist patiently and consistently offers empathic concrete reflections of the client's pre-expressive communication using Bodily, Situation, Word for Word, Reiterative and Facial Reflections.
- Client shows some change and response, whether it be their body position, facial expression or orally.
- Counsellor endeavours to acknowledge and communicate the change, striving to maintain contact.
- The beneficial effect may be that the client becomes aware of the therapist and a shared communication may develop, as well as a developing awareness of the shared reality.

Therapeutic process of Person centred counselling

- Two people willing to embark on a therapeutic relationship

- Both therapist and client have the ability to make contact and communicate with each other
- Therapist is non-directive, takes the client's lead.
- Client communicates something to the therapist.
- Therapist strives to understand how the client feels in their world and from their perspective.
- Counsellor receives the communication, is empathic to implicit and explicit feelings and congruently communicates back to the client what he received.
- Client receives the counsellor's communication, feeling heard and understood, and communicates his understanding along with a new communication back to the counsellor.
- Communication continues in this way and a therapeutic relationship has developed.

Understanding the history and development of Pre-Therapy gives an understanding of where Prouty's passion developed. The therapist appreciates that it is directive in order to be facilitative and recognises that it enables contact with someone who is limited in normal or usual realms of communication. Therefore, Pre-Therapy becomes 'a theory of Psychological Contact', the flexible pre-requisite to Rogers' hypothesised 'necessary conditions for a therapeutic relationship'.

CHAPTER 2:

EXPLORING PSYCHOLOGICAL CONTACT

The primary area of Prouty's development relates to Rogers' first therapeutic condition, Psychological Contact, and how is it achieved. This chapter examines, defines and establishes why Psychological Contact is a necessary requirement in the therapeutic relationship.

Regarding his first hypothesised condition, (Rogers, 1957) explanation of Psychological Contact is that "two people are to some degree in contact, that each makes some perceived difference to the experiential field of the other." However, lack of clarification around this seems to be the cause of limitations within the Person-Centred approach when working with clients who exhibit absence of autonomous communication skills.

A therapeutic relationship is a healing connection; one that has a good effect on body and mind; in this instance, one created between counsellor and client.

What exactly is Psychological Contact?
The first step to understanding Rogers' condition is to understand the meaning of the words 'psychological' and 'psychology'. The following are Concise Oxford Dictionary definitions.

Psychological
1. *Of, affecting, or arising in the mind.*
2. *Relating to psychology.*
3. Psychology

Psychology

1. *The scientific study of the human mind and its functions.*
2. *The mental characteristics or attitude of a person.*
3. *The mental factors governing a situation or activity.*

Therefore, Psychological Contact will be an effect in the mind of clients due to mental factors of attitude and situation.

The second step would be the realisation that in some instances, Rogers simply uses the word 'contact' when referring to Psychological Contact. Differentiating between the two words 'contact' and 'communication' will provide clarity.

Contact

1. *State or condition of touching or communicating with*
2. *Come across, meet.*

Communicate

1. *Share or exchange information or ideas.*
2. *Pass on, transmit, or convey (an emotion, disease, heat, etc.).*

Consequently, contact is the involvement of another person or persons in relation to one's self; communicating verbally, such as a conversation or utterances like tutting or sighing, or non-verbally, such as winking or a touch. Cameron (2001) states that there are four areas of contact:

1. Basic: acknowledgment.
2. Cognitive: understanding.
3. Emotional: having an emotional response.
4. Subtle: at some organic level, between the client and therapist, between body and mind.

Interestingly, Mearns (1996) states, "Most of human relating does not take place at depth." Rogers' (1980) mentions working "at a very deep level of intensity", thereby suggesting that 'deep' and 'depth' are significant when exploring Psychological Contact.

From the findings, four things are very significant at this point:

1. There has to be a sharing of communication with another person; a giving and a receiving.
2. The communication can be verbal or non-verbal.
3. The content will be of mental attitude, emotion, behaviour or thought.
4. The communication has to be more than surface level.

Investigating further, Rogers (1980) explains, "When I relax and be close to the transcendental core of me..."

Transcendental

1. *Relating to a spiritual realm.*
2. *Transcending normal or physical human experience.*
3. *(Of God) existing apart from and not subject to the limitations of the material universe.*

Could the transcendental core of Rogers be his spiritual core? This fits with other therapists' views. Professor Brian Thorne (2002) believes that God is the core of each one of us, that we are interrelated. Therefore, we are relational beings and we need each other for healing. Thorne feels this is what Rogers meant when he said "My inner spirit has reached out and touched the inner spirit of another" (1980). Rogers also uses the term 'a yearning for the spiritual' (1986). Is Psychological Contact, then, the spiritual or transcendental communication between two people?

Spiritual

1. *Of or concerning the spirit as opposed to matter.*
2. *Concerned with sacred or religious things; holy; divine; inspired (the spiritual life; spiritual songs).*
3. *(Of the mind, etc.) Refined, sensitive, not concerned with the material.*
4. *(Of a relationship, etc.) Concerned with the soul or spirit, etc., not with external reality (his spiritual home).*

For some, spiritual may qualify what Rogers' meant but not all hold this view. Professor Dave Mearns (2002), while acknowledging that the term 'spiritual' has taken on a wider meaning over the years other than to be associated with the religious dimension, respectfully avoids using the term so as not to offend those who believe that something larger than ourselves is core to our being.

Instead, Mearns talks of "intensifying human experiences", and he freely uses the term 'existential'. He speaks of being in touch with our own humanity and the humanity of others. He sees the connection of both of these as being the existential core of a person and calls this connection 'relational depth'; a secular language to describe a powerful phenomenon. Mearns believes that 'we', our 'self', the human person, is the highest form of entity; we are the core of our being.

Due to the fact that Rogers was a pioneer in the person-centred approach and because of the thoroughness of his research, there is reason to believe that he would not be solely satisfied with spiritual as his meaning of Psychological contact. He would "have been equally interested in the theoretical and empirical exploration of the phenomenon he observed" (Mearns, 1997).

Phenomenon

1. *A fact or occurrence that appears or is perceived, especially one of which the cause is in question. A remarkable person or thing.*
2. *The object of a person's perception; what the senses or the mind notice.*

Hence, Psychological Contact being a perception would indicate that it is relative to personal belief and experience, so to get a wider view of these perspectives opening up the subject of Psychological Contact with counselling professionals in various settings, provoked very deep conversations and led to many personal definitions offered below:

"Psychological Contact is deep and satisfying; it changes as feelings deepen between my client and myself."

"Well, I know, as does the client, that Psychological Contact is present because we feel it. The client may nod their head or give me a look that tells me I am spot on, and I will know it."

"Transference of deep empathy."

"It's a mystery; it's not black and white; it feels affective; it's just a knowing inside."

"Psychological Contact is a growth in the atmosphere where I connect with my client; the significant link that moves in and out, from one to the other."

"Rather than try describing Psychological Contact, I find it clearer to say it is blatantly obvious when it is not there. When one is not engaged psychologically, the therapeutic relationship has one massive unproductive hole in it."

"A reaching to the inner depth of the other person; a different level; a different degree of intensity in connection with the client." "A phenomenon" (Mearns, 1996).

Left with no doubt as to the therapists' awareness, does the client know when they are in Psychological Contact, and how do we interpret this?

"Now I know that you know, what I know, what I've always known. And now I know that you felt how I felt because I saw you feel it. I felt you feel it too. Now I know that you know how I feel, it's okay, because all I ever wanted was for one person in the whole world to understand, and you do." (taken from a taped session)

"I felt like you touched me somehow; I just feel like we did it together." (verbal feedback)

"Just passed around like a parcel. Yep, how did you know? Just like a parcel, just passed around. How did you know?" (8-year-old child)

"I knew that you knew all along, because your eyes kept telling me and I felt it, but I couldn't say. But it helped me because I knew you knew. I just had to wait until I was 16 and I felt you waiting with me." (letter to therapist some months after counselling had finished)

"I have never felt so emotionally understood."
(feedback form)

At the beginning I honestly thought you were a mind
reader." (feedback form)

"It felt as though he (the therapist) was right there, in
the garden, with me, like he could see it as well."
(Mearns & Dryden, 1989)

"I knew he felt my terror. But it wasn't just that; it was
one of those, I knew he knew I knew things. Like we
were communicating at a lot of different levels at the
same time." (Mearns & Dryden, 1989)

"There were a lot of silences. But 'silences' isn't a
word that I would like to use. It felt like, at points, it
was unbearable. The amount of emotion and the
intensity of the interaction between us." (Mearns,
1994)

"Some of the time, I felt like there was an angel in the
room touching all the parts that a human can't even
know about. I guess that she was an earth angel, if there
is such a thing." (verbal feedback)

"Sometimes something happens here, and it happened
again then, like I can't describe it." (from a supervision
session)

"Oh my God! That is so spooky! Spooky in a good
way, like, oh my God, did you get inside me?" (from a
15 year old)

Gathering terms from counsellors, clients and theorists, Psychological Contact can be any one or multiples of those listed below (not exhaustive). Research indicates that each description is subjective to the belief and experience of the individual.

Deep	A phenomenon	Transcendental Spiritual
Of the mind	Existential	Intensive
Felt	Satisfying	Humanity
Remarkable	Amazing	Relational depth
A mystery	Understanding	An experience
Growth	A significant link	Emotional
Knowing	Silence Incredible	Productive
Subtle	Real Genuine	Perceived
Enlightening	Done together	A sense
Effective	A connection	Varying communication levels

Definition of Psychological Contact

Psychological Contact is a phenomenological interaction, whereby two people sense each other at varying degrees of intensity as emotionally meaningful, thereby creating a link to the pivotal space where reception and transmission of deep exploration and understanding of the precise world of the other takes place; creating a significant healing connection.

The above seems quite long for a definition and, taking into account all the above discussions, it seems to me that, as a non-tangible, subjective matter, Psychological Contact is greater than the sum of all of its parts, and I wonder whether we're moving into the area of quantum mechanics.

Why is Psychological Contact a necessary requirement for a therapeutic relationship?

Psychological Contact paves the way for the client to explore deeper implicit feelings where they feel safe and accepted. Importantly, Rogers (1957) stated, "A therapist might experience a considerable depth of Psychological Contact with one client, a much more superficial contact with another and indeed a sporadic loss of contact with a third"; leading us to understand that the relationship is productive as long as an element of Psychological Contact exists.

The following passage is a therapeutic experience with a 16-year-old male client.. He had not spoken to me since our initial contracting. After every session with Dominic, I felt perplexed. In my process notes, I wrote, 'He uses the space well but I haven't a clue what's going on!' Having self-referred through his school pastoral manager, the form simply said:

> Dominic would like to go on the waiting list for counselling as he has nightmares and some problems due to his past life in his homeland and the transitional journey to the UK, which he said was very bad. He came to the UK when he was 10. I don't see any symptoms in school from Dominic; he is achieving as expected, seems to have a few friends and is on the football team.

Within supervision, I explored the lack of verbal communication within our sessions, which led me to realise that there were two differences in Dominic's activities. There were some instances of animation with Lego, the sand-tray and animal figures used symbolically, where he did speak perhaps a word or two in what I presumed to be his mother tongue. Occasionally, throughout his activities he would give me a scant glance but I was not invited to join in. Any words seemed intrusive; any empathic reflection ignored.

In contrast, sometimes he would sit on the floor or lie on his belly, moulding modelling clay, and he would 'zone out'. He did not respond if I spoke, unless I indicated that we only had a few moments left, whereby he would rub his face, stand up, nod at me and make his way towards the door.

Exploring if or not I was useful to Dominic in the sessions baffled me. Clearly, the sessions were useful to him some of the time, as seen through his animated play. However, what about during those times when he zoned out? When my supervisor suggested that we explore the level of Psychological Contact, this threw me completely. For somebody who would say that Psychological Contact was the key to therapy, I was unable to recount even one moment with Dominic.

From this supervision, I took with me the knowledge that, although I was in the room, I was not 'with' Dominic in a therapeutic way, and I would try and gain some level of contact.

Session 6

Lying on his belly, Dominic was quite engrossed in moulding some modelling clay, and I sat down on the floor opposite him. I watched him for a while, wondering what to do to change the pattern of previous sessions so that I could 'be with him'. I felt that I needed to do something to which he would respond. Not necessarily acknowledgement of my presence but more to communicate to him that I was there for him and whatever was inside him, and that I would recognise that he understood this by him giving some sign of response, no matter how small. This would fulfil both Conditions 5 and 6 of Rogers' therapeutic conditions.

What I didn't need in the room was Dominic picking up any of my anxiety, so I became aware of my breathing and thought how to make Psychological Contact. Closely observing, I could see just how involved he was in what he was doing. I could see the rise and fall of his back as he breathed in and out, the top of his jet-black wavy hair and the movement of his shoulders as he worked the clay. I couldn't feel any emotion in the atmosphere, and recall thinking, how can I paraphrase or empathise if I am not getting any emotional content? Then I remembered a quote from Rogers: "Simply my presence is releasing and helpful" (1980).

With this in mind, I tried to let go of 'thinking' and move to a more present state, but in a way in which Dominic could see me. I lay down on the floor facing him, to act as a reflection, which, I thought, was maybe the silent version of a paraphrase.

Seeing that he had shaped and separated some pieces of clay and had placed them down, I too moulded a piece of clay and placed it gently near to his pieces. Dominic pushed it out of the way and sighed. I clearly knew that I had intruded, and the atmosphere went cold. However, two things were apparent: my interaction had been acknowledged even if it was by intrusion; and I felt an emotion from Dominic.

I retrieved the rejected piece of clay. As I lay watching, almost tasting, the earthy smell from my hands, a guided meditation from a yoga class that had really moved me entered my awareness. It was simply to relax, listen to my breathing and connect to the mat that I lay on. As I did this, I had felt secure. I felt as though I had melted and the two had become one – mat and self – moving and being together in unison. Then the new unity connected with the floor, then the other people, the building, the road, the world, the universe and so on, until I was everything and everything was me;

not only physical but emotional; all. This feeling of completeness
had stayed with me for a few days.

I received the message that it may be healing to become one
with Dominic, so I listened again to his breathing, and shuffled my
position to almost parallel rather than in front of him. I could not
see his face, even though I was low to the ground, because he kept
his head bent and slightly turned away from me. I felt tranquil and
I noticed that our breathing pattern had synchronised. I felt a gentle
connection to him; a sense of comfortable similarity.

I became engrossed in watching him, and noticed little things,
like how he was twisting the clay rather than moulding it, and how
he flattened the bottom of the clay on the back of his hand, using
his nails to add details. The pieces did not represent anything to me
but I could tell that they were very precious to Dominic. I began to
do the same as him, but, instead of putting my finished pieces near
his, I kept them separate yet within his peripheral vision.

Very soon, we were both engrossed; he in his work and I as a
reflection. We worked in this way for quite a while. There was a
growing intensity of emotion in the atmosphere. As I focused
solely on Dominic, noticing that his breathing was shallower, my
vision blurred slightly and the room around us faded. To this day,
I could not explain how but quite suddenly I felt a block of fear
deep inside me, which I knew was not my fear. Acting on impulse,
I formed a clay shape quite different from the others, which I placed
just to the side of his, just within eye contact.

I felt prickly all over and shivered. I was aware of the need to
cry, and I felt a tear form but not fall. Then Dominic nodded,
nodded again and shook his head. He took the clay I had moulded
and fit it into his own group. The atmosphere reflected the
connection between us, within the space we now shared. I felt
completely at one with this young man, boy even, and it seemed
that he was with me. Everything around us was superfluous.
Dominic raised his head, tears streaming his face, his body shook

and he made a cry filled with pain and torment. He then clenched his fists and smashed every piece of clay, sat up, gathered the clay and threw it with full force to the wall. He howled again, piercing the air. I had knelt up to give him space to throw the clay and was moving backwards when he collapsed into a ball and rested his head in my lap. He trembled and shook. He sobbed choking, guttural sobs, gasping between each one. Crazy though this is, and with all the knowledge of safeguarding and the touch policy in school, my instinct was to stroke his head like one would a distressed infant, moving slowly. This is what I did. I felt the pain that he felt and, although not a tear left my eyes, I felt overwhelmed physically and emotionally. I knew that I had met deep Psychological Contact!

To answer the question of Psychological Contact being important to the therapeutic relationship, this example clearly shows that when there was no Psychological Contact the relationship was not meaningful; on initiation of Psychological Contact, therapy began.

Facilitation of Psychological Contact

As established, Psychological Contact is a two-way experience. From Rogers' other hypothesised conditions – congruence, empathy and unconditional positive regard, and with emphasis on the ability and willingness from both counsellor and client to engage – the transcript and evaluation below shows the therapeutic conditions working together.

The client was a woman in her early 30s, earlier sessions had related to the client's anxiety, panic attacks and feelings around her divorce. This was our sixth session together and the client had been discussing her feelings around son, who had learning difficulties and was finding school hard.

Client (1) "He is difficult at school too and, um, I just thought about Gemma then. He's going on a behaviour chart"

Therapist (1) "Sorry?"

Client (2) "School are putting him on a behaviour chart."

Therapist (2) "No sorry, it's just that I caught a feeling but didn't hear what you said, you said it fast and quiet and I almost missed it but who did you think of just then?"

(A pause in talking, atmosphere full of pain, client's face distorting and her chin wobbling, eyes filling with tears)

Client (3) "Gemma is my little girl that died." *(spoken very softly)*

Therapist (3) "Oh! So, Gemma, she just came into your mind?" *(mirroring the tone of client's voice)*

Client (4) "Mmm, she did last week *(biting her lip)*, but it was at the end of the thing when we were finishing, so I didn't bother mentioning it." *(rubs her eye and holds back tears)*

Therapist (4) "Okay, but she is here again. She has come back again. Sounds like it's, seems like it's having a real effect on you. Gemma's come back. I can see …"

Client (5) "I don't know what to say though." *(looking me straight in the eye, shaking her head and shrugging her shoulders)*

Therapist (5) *(I nod)* "But it hurts. Almost, there are no words to express…"

Client (6) *(Sobs)*

Client (1)	Mid-sentence, the client gave an indication of an implicit thought, feeling, emotion, so quietly and fast that she barely acknowledged it and carried on as if there had been no interruption in the process.
Therapist (1)	I felt alerted. The client spoke so quietly that I could not make out what she said but, from the fleeting gentleness of her voice and her expression, I could tell it was something important that had caught her off guard, and I was congruent to address this.
Client (2)	Almost an unawareness of what she had said, pushed it away and carried on as normal.
Therapist (2)	Congruent and empathic response. This felt so important, the feeling in me was, whoa, slow down! I need to hold this moment. The pause in talking was the pivotal point where Psychological Contact deepened. It was the unsure place where neither the client nor I knew where we were going.
Client (3)	In this moment, the implicit became explicit, where the client's subconscious pushed through and Gemma came into the room.
Therapist (3)	I gently offered back my willingness to be with her in her exploration. In this space, I felt

like I was holding Psychological Contact and was inviting the client to stay. It felt very fragile, and I could sense some trepidation from the client.

Client (4)   The client received the invitation and we stayed in Psychological Contact, more implicit feelings surfacing as she bit her lip, rubbed her eyes and held back her tears.

Therapist (4)   I held the Psychological Contact in this moment as I offered the client a mirror for her to see and feel her own pain and emotion that experiencing Gemma brought her.

Client (5)   Explicitly offered her inability to explain how she felt; implicitly tells of the depth of her pain, her desperation and vulnerability, her eyes plead with me. We connected on a deeper level of Psychological Contact. I felt it, and I know my client felt it too. There is a greater understanding here than words.

Therapist (5)   I attempted to put into words what the client has told me implicitly, on a psychological level, that I can feel her pain, and I understand that no words could ever explain how she feels.

Client (6)   The client's feelings overwhelm her. Her implicit feelings are now explicit. The client has received through Psychological Contact what she needed in order to begin her therapeutic journey of expressing her pain.

Psychological Contact facilitated the implicit subconscious feelings and allowed them to surface. Exploration could begin once they became explicit.

The reader will now not only have an understanding of psychological contact and the importance it holds in a therapeutic relationship, they will also understand the difference between implicit and explicit feelings and the importance of what is not being said. These non-tangible conditions, when teamed together do become tangible on an emotional level and when bonded they create movement in the therapy.

PRE-THERAPY

CHAPTER 3:

"Pre-Therapy is a theory of Psychological Contact"

(Prouty, 1990)

The development of Pre-Therapy came about primarily from working with clients who are 'contact impaired'; an old term not used very much today, meaning individuals for whom initiating social contact is difficult or people with low functioning abilities, whether this be a condition that individuals have been born with or one developed due to mental health difficulties.

At this point, it is worth recapping that this chapter looks at Pre-Therapy as a therapeutic intervention between a client who is in a state of incongruence, therefore showing elements of distress, and a therapist who is in a state of congruence. These are Rogers' hypothesised condition. Pre-Therapy is made up of:

CONTACT REFLECTIONS

which facilitate

CONTACT FUNCTIONS

which facilitate

CONTACT BEHAVIOURS

Contact Reflections (CR) are very simple, precise, concrete reflections. The aim is for the therapist to reach out and make contact with the client. There are five such reflections, as follows.

1. Situation Reflections (SR)

These refer to the immediate world around the client, the real world, the shared world of night and day, environment and other people. For example:

> "The sun is shining."
> "The door is closed."
> "There is a green car on the drive."
> "Mary is sitting in the chair."
> "David is playing with the cars."
> "It is Wednesday afternoon."
> "The radio is playing music."

Their function is to enable reality contact. To enable the client to experience contact with the real world around them, bringing an awareness of where they are, who and what is around them.

2. Facial Reflections (FR)

These refer to the facial expressions of the client. These are often pre-expressive feeling reflections and can be spoken or copied by the therapist. For example:

> "You are biting your bottom lip."
> "You are looking at my eyes."
> "You look sad."
> "Your teeth are clenched."

"You are shaking your head."
"You look puzzled."

Their function is to enable affective contact; allowing the client to come into contact with their own emotions and feelings.

3. Word for Word Reflections (WWR)

These refer to the reflection from the therapist of exact words spoken by the client, even if the therapist has no understanding of them. Sometimes a person in distress or in a pre-expressive state may shout, utter or just say things that may seem irrelevant to others, or they may say illegible words or make strange sounds. By the therapist copying these or saying them out loud, the client may actually hear themselves for the first time or feel like they have been understood; rather like a reaction to a paraphrase. For example, the client may say, "It's inevitable." The therapist would reflect precisely, "It's inevitable." If the client said, "Square boxes are dangerous," the therapist would reflect this word for word.

Their function is to promote communicative contact, to encourage the client to begin verbal communication.

4. Body Reflections (BR)

These reflect the client's own body position, which can sometimes be quite bizarre. The therapist can either verbalise the body position or take on the position themselves. For example:

"Your hand is on the top of your head."
"Your body is curled up."
 "Your legs are crossed."

Their function in theory is to help the client become aware of their own body and to gain conscious control over it.

These refer to the using again of any of the contact reflections, SR, FR, WWR and BR that have had any effect on the client. Their function would be to maintain or to strive to gain some level of contact towards the experience that the client is having in the here and now.

There is no order in which to apply these reflections but, when used together, they, "provide a web of Psychological Contact" (Prouty, 1998).

As mentioned above the use of Contact Reflections will lead to Contact Functions.

Contact Functions

Contact Functions (CF) refer to the client's process while in Psychological Contact; the client in the here and now; the shared reality. There are three CFs, as follows:

Reality Contact (RC)

Refers to the real, shared world and environment around the client. People, places, time, the weather and what is happening.

Refers to the client's awareness of his or her own moods, emotions, feelings and body positions. Not necessarily the reason for having them but for the client to acknowledge them.

Refers to the communication of being in the world, the client's communication of how they fit in the world and how they respond to it and other people. CC is usually verbal, or a shared, understood way of communicating, for example, hand signing for the deaf. "The symbolisation of reality (world) and affect (self) to others" (Prouty, 2002).

The development of these CF in psychotherapy leads the way towards enabling Psychological Contact with the client. This is the turning point in the client-counsellor relationship; the client communicates back to the therapist. The client shares their reality and the therapist joins them at this point. "Contact functions are the necessary conditions of psychotherapy" (Prouty, 2002)

Then as we learn above, Contact Functions lead to Contact Behaviours

Once the client has made contact with his/her own functioning, RC, AC and CC, they will then show some behaviour changes. These behaviour changes are known as Contact Behaviours (CB), as follows.

Social words and sentences

Facial and bodily expression
An awareness of other people, places and things
An ability to communicate with others

These behaviours become more logical as they develop. These adjustments within the client are the shift from a pre-expressive to an expressive state.

Evaluating the case study below shows the development of Psychological Contact with a client who is in such a state of distress they have become unable to communicate.

The client was at home in the basement of the family home where he had kept himself for some considerable months. He had deteriorated into psychosis and had no contact with anyone, creeping out at night to eat from the refrigerator. His feet were blue from lack of circulation and lack of movement. The client was in a severe catatonic state.

The therapist had been trying to make Psychological Contact with the client for an hour and half; SR and verbal BR had been given at five-minute intervals. During this time, the client had sat with his arms outstretched; his eyes were staring straight ahead and he was very rigid. In the hour and half the client had made no response and no movement. No Psychological Contact had taken place.

During the next section of the session, the counsellor 'brought her chair and sat directly in front of the client and mirrored his body exactly as she saw it'.

Transcript

Counsellor   "Your body is very rigid. You are sitting on
               the couch and not moving." (BR)

34

	(*15–20 mins later*)
	"I can no longer hold my arms outstretched. My arms are tired." (SR)
Client	(*No response. No movement*)
Counsellor:	"Your body is very stiff." (BR)
Counsellor:	"Your arms are outstretched." (BR)
Counsellor:	"Your body isn't moving." (BR)
Client:	(*Puts his hands on his head, as if to hold his head, and speaks in barely a whisper*) (AC) (AC) "My head hurts me when my father speaks." (CC)
Counsellor:	My head hurts me when my father speaks." (WWR)
Counsellor:	(*Puts her hands up as if to hold her head*) (BR)
	(*Some 4 hours later*)
Counsellor:	"It's evening. We are in the lower level of your home." (SR)
Counsellor:	"Your body is very rigid." (BR)
Counsellor:	"Your hands are holding your head." (BR)
Counsellor:	"My head hurts when my father speaks." (RR/WW)
Client:	(*Immediately drops his hands to his knees and looks directly into the counsellor's eyes*) (RC)
Counsellor:	"You've dropped your hands from your head and placed them on your knees. You are looking right into my eyes." (BR/FR)
Client:	(*Sits motionless for hours*)
Counsellor:	"You dropped your hands from your head to your knees." (RR/BR)
Counsellor:	"You are looking straight into my eyes." (FR)

Client:	*(Immediately speaks in a barely audible whisper)* "Priests are devils." (CC)
Counsellor:	"Priests are devils." (WWR)
Counsellor:	"Your hands are on your knees." (BR)

This is only part of the whole vignette, which in total lasted twelve hours (Prouty & Kubiak, 1988).

Evaluation

By placing her chair directly in front of the client, the therapist put herself directly in the client's line of vision, should he become able to see her. Because the client was staring straight ahead, it wasn't known whether or not he could see the therapist or indeed if he was seeing something in his imagination or could not see at all. From this angle, the therapist would be able to reflect the client's body movements more accurately; exactly like a mirror.

Taking up the same position as the client, holding her arms outstretched, sitting as he did and verbalising his body position, the therapist was not only using BR but was in fact going to the client's frame of reference. In his distress, the client could not verbally explain his frame of reference; he was, however, showing it.

Reflections of the fact that they were in his home, on the lower level, were used to remind the client where he was: the shared reality.

Not being sure whether the client could see her or hear her, the therapist's actions were reinforced by verbal communication. When the therapist's arms became tired and she put them down, she told the client why she had done this. There would be a chance, if the client could hear, that he would become aware of himself holding his arms outstretched, how very difficult that is to maintain, and perhaps register that he had been doing that for a considerably long time. She was striving to promote AC.

Contact was made. This was shown when the client placed his hands on his head and spoke of his father. The CC shows some acknowledgement that the client is aware of the therapist's presence.

Further on, by using RR, BR, WWR and FR, the client responded by moving his arms and making eye contact with the therapist and eventually making verbal communication.

The above shows that CR facilitate CFs. The CFs are as follows:

> 1. The client putting his hands down: AC.
> 2. The client speaking: CC.
> 3. The client staring straight into the therapist's eyes: RC.

Confirming that CF facilitate CB is the fact that, shortly after this episode, the behaviour of the client changed: he was able to walk around the farm, talk in everyday communication, book himself air tickets and travel to a residential centre for treatment.

There were six stages in the process of this therapeutic intervention, as follows:

> 1. The counsellor was unable to make contact with the client.
> 2. The client was unaware of anyone, including counsellor, and was in his own reality.
> 3. The counsellor patiently and consistently strove to make contact with client.

4. The client received some contact and showed some response.
5. The counsellor endeavoured to communicate his acknowledgement of this response still using the reflections, striving to maintain contact.
6. The client came back with the counsellor to the shared reality.

Did Pre-Therapy facilitate Psychological Contact?
By understanding the depth of distress that the client showed through his catatonia and inability to communicate, to fulfil Condition 5 of Rogers' therapeutic conditions, the therapist showed empathy by using CR. When the client spoke words that made no sense to the therapist, these words were reiterated, marking important points towards facilitating CF. The therapist could not be more empathic than to strive to enter, unconditionally, the frame of reference of the client, in his world, of which the therapist had no understanding. In this instance, the 'being with' the client facilitated Psychological Contact. As defined earlier:

> Psychological Contact is a phenomenological interaction of minds between two people sensing each other as emotionally meaningful, communicating at varying degrees of intensity, creating a significantly healing connection.

The level of intensity in which the therapist and client communicated was significantly healing, therapeutic enough certainly for the client to return safely to the shared reality. He regained full control over his body, his behaviour, his ability to communicate and his ability to relate to the world around him, functioning as he did in everyday life.

The therapist may not have understood the meaning of the client's words, but Psychological Contact does not mean understanding of content; it is an emotional phenomenon. If Psychological Contact had not been made, there would still be no response from the client.

Whereby the therapist spent twelve hours working with the above client due to the severity of his catatonia, milder situations can also benefit from the use of Pre-Therapy. The example below took place in a mainstream school.

Jake

Sadly for Jake, school was an unhappy place to be. He found it difficult to communicate and understand other pupils, staff and the school routine. Consequently, some days he cried and talked about wanting to die. Jake's tears were often from pure frustration because he clearly did not understand the teachers. In return, the teachers did not understand Jake. Within the last month, Jake had been given a statement for support in school and was diagnosed as having Asperger's syndrome. He was in a period of transition awaiting placement at a school more suited to his needs.

Passing the sports corridor, I heard quite a commotion. One of the male teachers was shouting at a group of boisterous Year 7 boys piling out of the changing room. Turning to me, one of the boys said, "Oh, Mrs Smith, you should go in there. I think Jake needs you."

On entering, the teacher concerned looked totally worn out and pointed to Jake. "He's been there for the whole sports lesson, like that, and he's still like that now! I don't know what to do. I'm going to phone his parents!"

"Okay," I said. "I'll stay with him, see what I can do."

I tried at first being gentle and asking what the matter was but there was no response. I knew Jake fairly well. I understood him most of the time, and when he was finding things tough around school he was allowed to come and find me. He had a copy of my timetable. I felt that Jake trusted me.

Standing on the bench in the changing room, with his knees bent, Jake's arms were stretched right up and he was gripping so tightly with one hand on to the bar on the storage racks and with the other on to a coat hook that his knuckles had turned white. I could not see his face because his head was bent low and against the wall. When I visualised what it must be like to hold my body in that way and realised that Jake had been in that position for more than an hour and fifteen minutes, I realised just how distraught he must be. That's when I decided to use Pre-Therapy. I toyed with the idea of mirroring Jake's position but decided against it because he would not have been able to see me and the coat hooks didn't look that strong, so, instead, I sat on the bench leaning backwards, trying to look upwards towards his face.

Me:	"Jake, you are in the changing room at school." (SR)
Jake:	(*No response*)
Me:	"Jake, you are in the changing room and you are standing on a bench." (SR/BR)
Jake:	(*No response*)
Me:	"Jake, you are holding on to the bar very, very, tightly. Your hands look sore." (SR/BR)
Jake:	(*No response*)
Me:	"Jake, I cannot see your face. You are in the changing rooms at school and your knuckles are white from gripping the bar so tightly. You are standing on a bench." (SR/BR)
Jake:	(*No response*)

I continued like this for another 5–10 minutes.

Me: "Jake, you are in the changing room in school, you have been here a very long time, your knuckles are white and you are standing on the bench. It is dinnertime." (SR/BR)
(Jake makes a high-pitched wailing noise) (AC)

Me: "I hear you crying." *(This was the best I could do for a WWR. I could not make the sound that Jake made but I let him know that I heard it)*

Jake: *(Silent)*

Me: "Jake, you are in the changing room. You made a crying noise." (SR/RR). *(I used RR here because I wanted to let Jake know that I had heard him; his noise was the beginning of CC).*
(Jake makes the same wailing noise again, only slightly louder) (AC)

Me: "I hear you. You make a noise, which sounds like crying or screaming." (WWR)
(Jake stops crying)

Me: "You cried, you sound upset. We are in the changing room at school; you are standing on the bench. It was sports lesson; now it's lunchtime." (WWR/SR)

Jake: "They're horrible, they're horrible, they're horrible, they're horrible!"*(Continues saying this for around 3– 4 minutes, in chant-like whine)*(CC)

Me: "They're horrible. They're horrible." (WWR)

Jake: *(makes the wailing noise again)* (AC)

Me: "Jake, I hear you crying, 'they are horrible'.
        They make you feel like climbing on the
        bench and holding on the bar until your hand
        hurts." (SR/BR/WWR)

Jake: *(Jake let's go of the bar and almost falls off
        the bench. The PE teacher, who had arrived
        back to the sound of Jake's wail, catches
        hold of him and turns him round so that he
        can sit on the bench. Jake grabs hold of the
        teacher's arm and sits on the bench, crying,
        chanting between breaths, "They're horrible,
        they're horrible", while moving his feet up
        and down on the floor).* (AC/ RC/CC)

Me: "They're horrible. They're horrible." (WWR)
        *(Jake continues crying and chanting until his
        voice becomes more audible and quieter)*

Me: "You are quieter now. You're okay now.
        There is nobody here but you, me and Sir.
        We are sitting in the changing room and you
        are holding on to Sir's arm." (SR/BR)

Jake   (M*akes the wailing noise again but not as
        loudly and for not as long)*

Me: "We are in the changing room at school and
        it is lunchtime." (SR)
        *(Jake begins whimpering; the kind of noise a
        child makes when they are finishing crying.
        Jake lets go of the teacher's arm)*

It was at this point I stopped using Pre-Therapy and moved into
congruent conversation because Jake was back with us, in the
changing room. He was less distressed and was becoming able to
communicate. Also, he was now at a point of distress from which

I had worked with him before and I knew that we would very soon be on a more even keel)

When he was, Jake told us about the incident that had caused him to climb on to the bench. Jake had gone through all the CFs until he was then able to change his contact behaviours. When he went for his lunch, he was back to being able to communicate and manage himself.

The above scenarios clearly show the process which occurs within a client once Pre-Therapy strategies are used. Justifiably, when in a state of shock, trauma or distress, people and the environment fade into the distance and energy resources are used for basic functioning.

Probably many will have experience of such a time; during a traumatic event, maybe when being told someone has died or some similar incident which causes shock.

In visual terms, it is rather like a man who has fallen into a treacherous sea. Using all his energy, he is only managing to keep his head above the waves. There is no way this man can swim to shore. In order to survive, he will need some assistance; maybe someone to rescue him in a boat or perhaps throw him a rope. So it is with someone in a state of mental distress. In order for them to survive more comfortably, someone needs to go to them at the point of their suffering. In the example, it would be no use if the person with the boat didn't get close enough to the drowning man or the man with the rope didn't throw it near enough.

In this instance, Pre-Therapy is the boat or the rope. It gets close enough to the distress so that the client can get hold of something – the empathy or the unconditional positive regard – and aid in their own rescue.

CHAPTER 4

OUT OF CONTACT

'Out of contact' is not as simple as meaning not in contact in the shared reality, being other people, the time of day and environment, but also means not in contact with anyone even about their own reality and experience.

For us to understand the value of Psychological Contact, we need to examine what out of contact feels like because it may be a presumption that the world of the client is uncomfortable. Looking at Rogers' Condition 5, Lisbeth Sommerbeck states that it is the therapist who is "missing a sense of 'empathic mutuality" (2006), therefore it is important to be sure that we are meeting a need in the client and not just the therapist.

I once met a lady, who was dancing and swirling down the corridor of the hospital, held by the paramedic who had brought her in. She was by her own account "on board the Titanic", having the time of her life, dancing and singing with all the officers, dressed in her flamboyant ball gown and surrounded by good company and luscious food. She stopped and curtsied in front of me and tried to link my arm in dance. Why not leave her there in the beautiful world she had created for herself? Sometimes, might the out of contact place of the client/patient be better than the mutually empathic place sought by the therapist?

Without doubt, all of us at some time have been out of contact with those around us. We will have experience of being 'miles away', daydreaming. A student may seem to have been looking and listening during the lesson but, when the teacher asks a question, the student does not answer or respond because they haven't heard the question and are not in fact looking or listening at all, but are daydreaming, thinking about something else entirely, completely unaware in that moment of their surroundings and peers. Maybe the teacher will bang on the table or the room will erupt with laughter that will bring the student's awareness back to the classroom; back to the here and now of shared reality. For a few seconds, the student may be bewildered, taking a moment to refocus, but within a few more seconds they will be back in contact and will be functioning normally. Certainly, this kind of brief dissociation is normal; many people experience it while driving, becoming aware that they have arrived at the destination but with no memory of roundabouts or traffic lights, and so on.

I recall having a coffee in a café with a friend. We had been chatting, when my friend put her coffee down, put her hands under her chin and seemed to drift off into space. I sipped my coffee and watched her. I made a comment, but it seemed that she didn't hear me. I waited a moment then said her name, but she still didn't respond. A moment or two later, without interruption, she came to focus on us both sitting in the café once again.

"What, uh, oh, sorry, pardon, what did you say?" she stammered.
"You okay?" I asked.
"Yeah. Sure," she replied.
"What were you thinking about?" I asked.
"Uh, oh, don't know. I was miles away." She shrugged.

For a moment we lost contact; my friend went 'somewhere else'.

Unquestionably, drug use, prescribed or non-prescribed, can affect someone in a way that causes loss of contact and awareness of the world around them. Having had an operation on my back, the doctor's words "Be very careful not to lie on your back and try not to bang it" echoed through my mind even though I was sedated and drifting in and out of sleep and awareness all the time. Somehow, I decided that I could walk, and further decided to take myself off to the toilet. I recall feeling dizzy and faint, and the doctor's words kept ringing in my head. All I could think was, if I fall, I'm going to bang my back. I saw a chair and headed for it. I thought I had sat down on it. Next thing, it seemed to me that the nurses were pushing me, trying to make me lie down, but I was afraid and I thought that I might bang my back on something, so I resisted all their efforts, too medicated to make coherent words.

Then I heard a voice saying, "Bernadette, it is okay. You are standing up. We are trying to sit you down in a wheelchair." That's when I became aware of the reality. I hadn't made it to the chair. I had passed out before getting there, and one of the nurses had caught me before I fell. In my haze, when I thought I was sitting, I was actually still standing. I was out of touch with the shared reality of the ward, all activity and even the realness of myself for a little while. What brought me back into reality was the nurse who told me where I was and what I was doing. She acted like a mirror, reflecting the reality to me. This is significant in Pre-Therapy.

Interestingly, de-stress and relaxation techniques actively encourage us to lose contact, in the form of meditations and visualisations. These mild dissociations are considered healthy and therapeutic. We have the control and ability to bring ourselves back into the shared reality at any time. The difference here is the ability to bring oneself back. When a person loses that ability, the being out of contact becomes a problem.

Understanding that 'loss of contact' can be due to a number of different factors and bearing in mind that episodes can last for varying lengths of time, we now focus on how that feels. It is very difficult for a person to try and explain how they felt when out of contact, because they must have regained contact in order to explain.

Clients' personal experiences

Recalling a period of being out of contact with the therapist

"I remember becoming completely isolated and separated from my counsellor. I was shivering and was unable to move or communicate. I couldn't make eye contact. I could see myself and the abuser. I was almost watching the whole thing take place in front of me. I could see him laughing, laying the trap. I wanted to turn my head but couldn't move. I wanted to say to my counsellor what I saw but I couldn't speak; I couldn't shift the image. I could hardly breathe. I felt paralysed. I was very scared of getting lost. I began to get very strong suicidal feelings. I seemed to have split into two. It was very scary, strange."

Recalling a long psychotic episode

"It might have kept me safe, but it was lonely, cold, wet and frightening. One move and I would have fallen; dead. That's how it felt. That's how I felt most of my life. That's how it felt with you at first; cold and not really real."

"Oh, I was just fine, soo happy, so beautiful. It is such a shame I had to come back to this. I want to live there forever."

Young person

"I think I got lost inside my head then, or in space."

Paul

"I could just about see my mum kneeling beside me. I couldn't form any words in my mind. My head filled with shapes and colours, so I couldn't speak. I couldn't move either; I was paralysed. Inside I was screaming for my mum to wake me up, but when she touched me I couldn't feel anything. I was separate from everything, like I was really heavy but floating."

Man in his 40s

"I have no idea. I know it happened but that's about all. I lost time somewhere though."

Determined from all but one of these examples, out of contact is a mixture of distressing emotions: lonely, cold, wet, frightened, disabled, paralysed, just a fall away from death, not really real, invisible, out of reach, scary, split, suicidal, strange, lost, separate, heavy, floating. Clearly not a comfortable place to be.

The dancing lady is quite the opposite. She clearly enjoyed her experience but her family and nursing staff felt very differently. The daughter and partner of this lady were distraught that they could not cope with such an extreme high. The episode had been building up for a few days, and she had made a lot of noise, disturbing neighbours in the early hours of the morning, shouting in the street. When the family tried to bring her inside, she fought them off. On admission, the paramedic said that he had to dance her to and from the ambulance and that she was so insecure on the journey that he had strapped her arms so that she didn't try to stand up. The nurse on the ward told me that she would come down eventually and then be the complete opposite, which she did. When I saw her a day or two later, she looked tired, grey, very sad and was slumped in her chair refusing food or drink.

Carers' and significant others' experiences

The mother of Paul in Example 5 above described the experience as being one of the most frightening of her life. "Paul was like the living dead. I was scared that Paul was dying or something. I couldn't reach him. I felt like he saw through me. I didn't understand what was happening to him. I didn't know how to help."

Sporadic loss of contact

As a teaching assistant, I supported a child aged around 8 who often 'blanked out'. During these episodes, he would continue what he was doing – working, playing, walking or eating – but it was as if he became deaf and totally unaware of others around him, with no response to verbal communication or other noise. The occurrences were strange.

If somebody held him, he would remain still, never struggling, showing no facial expression until they let go. After a while, he would join us again as if all were the same as before. He never seemed to show any concern or distress. I often wondered what he thought had happened when he had missed some instructions during a lesson or something similar but he never seemed fazed and never acknowledged these episodes. His parents, however, found the situation very distressing, and were understandably fearful. They did not dare allow the boy menial tasks, such as going out on the street alone, for fear that he would walk into the road and get knocked down. Neither could he be alone in the bath or swimming pool for fear of drowning if he went into a 'trance'.

Comments were made at these times such as "The lights are on but no one is home." Cruel comments from people who didn't understand. At the time, medical examinations had drawn a blank; tests having been carried out to see if this was a kind of epilepsy or abnormal brain functioning. When these came back as inconclusive, it was suggested by the profession that the difficulties were psychological. I pondered over where he went to in his mind, and why. I was often not in any form of Psychological Contact with this boy; again, leaving me wondering who was out of contact with who. We expected the child to stay in the shared reality, but how sad that nobody knew how to venture into his world.

Asperger's syndrome

Again. During my teaching assistant years, I supported an 11-year-old boy, who would squeeze his eyes tight shut, grimace and clench his fists while making a quiet screeching noise.

Clearly distressed, these episodes lasted from a few minutes up to two hours. While working with this child, there were many times when I couldn't reach him on a psychological level. I could not work out the triggers to his behaviour, and the child could not explain his distress in a way that I could understand. I felt out in the cold, useless and confused. I wondered who was out of contact with who. Was he out of contact with the shared reality or was his experiencing during those moments a reality that nobody was sharing? It brought me to thinking that we were both out of contact with each other, neither of us knowing how to get into contact with the other.

Hallucination

Doris, an educated woman and a highly respected leader of a large law firm, began seeing and talking to her mother, who had died some twenty years earlier when Doris was in her late 20s. Doris said that her mother had been away, but that she was back for a short while to sort out some family problems. Doris was in and out of hospital frequently during this two-year period, yet during the intervals in-between she managed to continue working and raising her family. A huge amount of Doris' upset was due to the fact that nobody else could see or hear her mother. She found this almost unbearable and, while she was delighted to have her mother around, she couldn't grasp the fact that it was a hallucination, because it was real to her. She felt betrayed by her loved ones.

Doris' husband and sister didn't know how to handle the situation. Her husband wasn't sure whether to watch while she talked to thin air or whether to try and stop her. He became anxious about being out with her in case she saw her mother, and found these occasions very distressing and embarrassing. After a particularly bad spell, Doris was admitted again on to the mental health ward where, one night, waking in the darkness, crying with grief, she told the nurse that her mother had woken her to say goodbye. Doris never saw her mother again and is now back to leading a normal life. She speaks of that period as her 'mother time' but looks back on it with mixed feelings. She fails to understand how it happened, is somewhat fazed by the whole thing and is a bit scared that it might happen again. However, she feels delighted to have been able to spend more time with her mother but sad that it wasn't real, although it was very real to her.

Therapists' experiences

Through supervision and in professional conversation with therapists, I have discovered that they too feel some level of discomfort when out of contact with their client.

"I just can't seem to reach him where I need to be. It feels like I am missing something really important."

"I think I need to refer the client somewhere because the work I am doing is unproductive."

"He behaves really strangely, closing his eyes half way, and then it is as if he disappears or as if he makes me disappear. This is happening for longer periods of time and I am worried that I might lose contact with him altogether. Then what would happen? Sometimes in those situations I feel really sad and helpless. I feel a bit desperate, to be honest."

"I'm with her and then I am not. I feel like laughing or crying. I don't know what is going on inside her, but she just loses me. I will try to gain contact and, just when it feels like I have met her, she moves again. Most of my notes are blank because there is nothing to write."

"He sat staring into space for almost an hour. I tried all sorts but I couldn't feel anything from him. I'm really stuck here. He is a private client. He comes weekly but I feel bad taking his money if I am not helping him."

"I strive to make Psychological Contact but she just shuts down. She sits with one foot tucked under her up on the chair, twisting her wedding ring round and round. I don't know if she is thinking at all. I have no idea what is going on in her; she goes blank. I notice she does make a little humming sound – maybe a tune – but it is so quiet I can't make it out. She does come back but we never pick up where we left off and she seems a bit vacant."

The reader can see that being 'out of contact' causes personal anguish and uncertainty for the client. Being lost in their self and not being able to communicate, the client is not aware of their own behaviour. They separate from the world we share and from their ability to interact within the realms of normal functioning, such as eye contact and conversation.

For professionals working with the client or for significant others who care about the client this can be stressful as it leads to the loss of a meaningful connection with the other person leading to a sense of personal helplessness.

CHAPTER 5:

<u>OBSERVING AND LEARNING</u>

Through observation I have come to find that Pre-Therapy CR's are simple and natural. Judging when to use them is a skill in itself.

Getting it wrong

When counselling a 35-year-old female client with Down's syndrome using regular person-centred therapy, Psychological Contact became sporadic, and my client would hold one elbow and put her free hand on the side of her face and seemingly drift off into space. After this had happened a few times, I mirrored her action, whereby, from the corner of her eye she looked shyly at me, turned her head towards me and said, "Why you doing that with your hand? You copying me?" "Mmm, I was just wondering how it felt when you do that," I replied. "Well, don't do that because you look really, really, silly. You want to know what it feels like, ask me. I won't shout at you," she invited. "I'm sorry. I was wondering how it felt when you do that, putting your hand to your face like that," I asked. "I don't know now how it feels because you've stopped me thinking." To which we both laughed. She tapped me on the arm and said, "You funny you."

I still laugh whenever I think about this. Lesson learnt!

Children at play

Much of my development has been through observing, children especially, who seem to perform the CR automatically. Often, these reflections are primitive, simplistic and intuitive.

54

Observing a group of 7 year olds during play, I noticed a sad little girl, who was sitting cross-legged and was alone in the corner of the playground. She had been there a few minutes when a young friend went up to her and cuddled her but she was shrugged off. One of the members of staff also went over to the girl, tried to talk to her but the child didn't respond. She kept her arms folded and her head turned away. A few minutes later, another child went towards her, didn't speak but sat down opposite her in the same position, legs crossed, arms folded, and head down. Within a minute, the two were up and running around. No great therapy but definitely contact; some non-verbal understanding of each other purely through body language.

Natural empathy

I have always had a willingness to observe and seek advice when stuck, taking difficulties to supervision, personal reflection or discussing with colleagues. However, sometimes the answers don't lie with the professionals.

Vini, a 10-year-old boy, looked forward all week to his sessions. Whenever he saw me around school he would chirp up with, "See you on Thursday." So I knew that these sessions were important to him. Vini had some communication and conversation difficulties; his behaviour and verbalising being quite mechanical. During our sessions, he used minimal speech and would nod or shake his head if I asked him a direct question. He would, however, wander around the room selecting different toys to communicate through, and loved role play with puppets. Our sessions lasted fifty minutes, and at the end of the session it was break time.

Working in a school, it was not possible to be flexible with time because everything runs to a structure. Every now and then I had playground duty, and children could not be left alone in a room. However, when the end of our session together approached, Vini became very stiff, as if glued to the spot. He would put his hands in his pocket and become solid and silent, almost to the point of shutting down.

I sensed an underlying unhappiness and maybe some fear, but I could not make contact with Vini in any of these areas. I wondered if he felt my tension and apprehension around getting to the playground on time. I tried different things for a few weeks: being gentle; being firm. I had begun a couple of sessions offering to work around making the ending of the session easier for him, about how I would let him know ten minutes before that it was nearly the end of our session. Although he nodded in agreement that he would go, when the time came he wouldn't, he couldn't, it was as if he became paralysed. On two occasions, I had left him in the room, telling him that I needed to go now and he had come down by himself, but always looking sad and agitated.

Thankfully, one day the room to my door was open as the break time bell sounded. Other children passing put their heads round the door to say "hi" and others just popped in to say "Miss I've done this" or "Miss I've done that." One of the girls, Chrissie, stopped. She came in and looked at Vini, then at me. Vini was standing with his head down and his hands in his pockets; he was rigid. He didn't see Chrissie as she entered and had not responded to any of the other children who had passed by.

Chrissie asked me with her eyes, not her voice, if I wanted Vini to go. I nodded; neither of us spoke. She walked over to Vini and stood by his side. She mirrored his body position exactly, putting her hands by her sides, as she had no pockets. She sighed deeply, and very gently put her arm round Vini, saying, "You're sad it's the end of your time with Mrs Smith, but it's break time. I'll walk down with you." Then she put her arm around his waist, manoeuvred him around, still with her head bent like his, and, matching his stuttering walk, she began very gently singing to him. He walked all the way down the stairs with her. While I was in the playground, I saw Vini playing with the other children; happy and back to being himself.

Chrissie knew naturally how to make contact with Vini, and I learnt a great deal from watching her. Her empathy lay in her mirroring Vini's body and verbalising her sense of his feelings. As our next session came to an end, I played some soft music to create a sense of relaxation. When the bell went and Vini put his head down and his hands in his pockets, I reflected, "You're sad it's the end of our time together for today," and, mirroring his stance, "Come, Vini, its break time," I very gently touched his arm and we walked down stairs together. Once in the food hall, Vini was fine and, as he joined his peers, he said with a smile, "See you next Thursday, Miss."

Striving to make contact

Much of my research has been around my own striving to facilitate contact between self and client, or for self to enter the world of another, displaying what I perceive to be contact difficulties. What I had not considered before until this moment was how one with perceived difficulties strives to gain contact with others around them.

A friend and her daughter, Kirsty, age 9, were visiting my home. Kirsty, who, along with other complex needs, didn't speak or walk, although she made guttural sounds, laughed and moved around by sliding along on her bottom. Occasionally, she would stand if there was someone or something to hold on to.

Kirsty could give the loveliest hugs at this age with a warm and loving smile. However, due to the complexities of her disability, she would acknowledges hurt by laughter, and have a tendency to throw things, kick, bite or head bang without warning. For the most part, it was very difficult to understand what she wanted and impossible to know what she was thinking. She would make contact if she wanted to, but it was difficult for others to make contact with her. Quite often, she was the most comfortable in her own world.

Attempting to make contact with Kirsty and to satisfy my own need for acknowledgement, I said "Hello", and was ignored. I put my arms out, offering a cuddle, and was again rebuffed. I sat on the floor next to her in order to gain some contact and mirrored her movements. I did gain some contact because she suddenly hit me in the face, knocking my glasses off. I clearly got the message that she didn't want contact with me at that moment.

Having occupied herself with a coloured ball for a while, Kirsty stopped and looked around the room, settling her eyes on my 12-year-old son, who was engrossed watching television. Kirsty was not interested in the television but she kept looking over to my son, who was unaware of her attention. After making some noises and getting no attention at all from him, she observed him for another moment, then slid her way over to the television, taking a look at him over her shoulder. Still my son showed no awareness of what she was doing. Kirsty put her arms around the sides of the television unit and pulled herself up, whereby she hugged the television and wiggled from side to side, therefore blocking his view. My son just moved his head round from side to side to see what he could between Kirsty's movements. He had no idea that she was trying to get his attention. Somewhere in the past, as a result of having been bitten, kicked or head banged, he had learnt to be very patient around her and not to bother her; just leaving her to do her own thing until she decided otherwise.

While continuing our conversation, my friend and I observed Kristy. She dropped herself on to the floor, slid on her bottom across the living room to the settee where my son was and sat on the floor in front of him for a few minutes. My son, his body slouched, his elbow on the arm of the settee propping up his head, was still staring at the television; still completely oblivious of Kirsty's attempts to get his attention.

What happened next was really quite amazing. Kirsty knelt up, leant on the settee next to him, put her elbow out and propped her head up in her hand, mirroring his position as best she could. My son then saw her and said, "Hello Kirsty. Are you copying me? Do you want to play?"

Kirsty had made contact purely through bodily reflection.

CHAPTER 6:

A WORKING RELATIONSHIP WITH PRE-THERAPY IN EVERYDAY THERAPEUTIC PRACTICE

Pre-Therapy is now integral to my work. Whereas Prouty's work related to seriously regressed clients, and Van Werde's to the better functioning psychotic clients, where he explores the area of 'grey-zone contact', my work is a continuum of this but with clients with no mental health diagnosis who may be attending mainstream education or have self-referred for counselling, either in private practice or through a charitable organisation. I draw upon Pre-Therapy whenever and wherever the situation arises. I find myself using the techniques alone or mixed with original person-centred therapy during the therapeutic hour with a client or also (and hugely successfully) in the here and now, on the spot; sometimes in crisis management.

On the brink

In mainstream high school, 14-year-old Simon would sometimes be found in the corner of a corridor or under a table, curled up almost in the foetal position or sitting with his knees under his chin and his arms wrapped around his legs, head down and eyes half open. On occasions, he made a gentle humming noise; other times, it seemed more of a mutter; and sometimes he was silent. Episodic time spans varied: one teacher reporting ten minutes; another, forty-five minutes. There did not seem to be a specific trigger to this behaviour.

Simon had little idea of why this happened. When he came out of one of his episodes, he did not seem to understand what had gone on, and he certainly lost awareness of time.

I was relatively newly qualified as a counsellor at this time and the Special Needs Coordinator in school had included me as part of Simon's support on his individual behaviour plan. A referral to the educational psychologist had been made and my work was in the interim to the request. I was told that Simon's behaviour was relatively new because in his first two years in school this had not happened, and it was a puzzle why it had started happening now.

I had begun using Pre-Therapy with Simon at these times because he became non-respondent and non-communicative; clearly out of contact. It seemed to me that he had left the shared reality of everyday life in school and was in his own reality; a reality he could not express other than curling himself up out of everybody's way.

On this particular morning, Simon had simply put his equipment down, walked out of the classroom, sat in the corner of the corridor and curled up. He must have been there for more than ten minutes because a pupil had to come and find me in another area of school.

Me:	(*I knelt beside Simon; there was no way I could physically get into the same position*) "You are all curled up like a tiny baby." (BR)
Simon:	(*No response*)
Me:	"You are sitting in the corner of the corridor in the maths block." (SR)
Simon:	(*No response*)
Me:	"Your eyes are almost closed." (*I wait for two or three minutes before saying anything else,* *during which time I try to get my head and eyes on* *a level with Simon's*) (BR)
Simon:	(*No response*)

Me: "You are not looking at anything. You are shutting
           everything out." (BR)
           (*Simon blinks, quickly glances at me then turns his
           head to the wall. He stays like that for a minute or
           two*)
Me: "You glanced at me and then turned your face to
           the wall."
Simon: (*No response*)
Me: "You glanced at me then turned your face to the
           wall. You are trying to shut me out."
           (*I very powerfully feel Simon trying to block
           contact and so use a congruent response*) (FR/BR)
Simon: (*Sighs*)
Me: "You sighed deeply." (WWR)
Simon: (*No response*)
Me: "You sighed deeply. You are trying to shut me out
           and your eyes are almost shut."
           (*I immediately feel a wave of anger from Simon
           even though he hasn't moved. I feel his emotion*)
           (*Slowly and precisely, Simon turns towards me
           with clenched teeth and glared at me with his eyes
           wide open. I am taken quite by surprise and know
           my expression had shown it*)
Me: "You are glaring at me. Your eyes are wide open
           and you look very angry and scary." (BR/FR)
           (*Simon continues glaring. However, the edge has
           gone. He has also changed his body position
           slightly and seems to relax a little*)
Me: "You are still glaring at me, but you don't look so
           scary anymore. I don't feel frightened now."
           (*As soon as I have said this, I wonder whether or
           not mentioning that I had been momentarily
           frightened was the right thing to say. However, it*)

*proves to be okay. On reflection, I realise that for a
moment I feared he would become violent. This
was an unrealistic fear, as Simon had never shown
any violence before)*

Simon: "But you did feel frightened, didn't you Miss?"
*(Simon moves out of his trance into a more
congruent relationship)*

Me: "Yes, I did. I did feel a bit scared for a second or
two back then when you looked very angry and
scary."

Simon: "I wanted to frighten you, but now I don't. It's
horrible to be frightened, isn't it, Miss?"

Me: "It seems like you find it horrible to feel
frightened?"

Simon: "Yes, Miss. I do. Do you?"
*(I look at Simon for a moment. I don't know for
certain where I am therapy wise: Pre-Therapy or
have I moved into therapy? It is a continuum;
congruence pushes itself forward and I say what I
feel needs to be said)*

Me: "Yes, Simon, I also find it horrible to feel
frightened. We both find it horrible to feel
frightened."

Simon: *holds eye contact with me for quite a few seconds. I
feel as though he is looking deep into me to see if I
am being honest with him, during which time his
face softens and the tenseness leaves his eyes.
After a few minutes, moves his gaze away from me,
stands up. Slowly,, looks out of the window, nods,
then turns back to me and nods again.*

Me *I nod back. Nothing else is said by either of us, but
I feel something change inside me. I feel as though
a whole weight has been lifted; so different and*

*sudden was the change I recall that I also felt
exhausted. Simon turns and goes back into class,
where he sits at his desk and continues with the
lesson*)

I feel that with the support from myself and, later, the support from the school counsellor, Simon's need to express his pain and confusion changed from pre-expressive, by curling up in the corridor and withdrawing, to expressive in the interactions with me and, later, the deeper conversations with the counsellor. I feel that, had the support not been to hand, Simon would perhaps have developed a more severe mental health issue.

Importantly, one point I would like to make is that by using Pre-Therapy techniques one is able to gain a deeper presence into the world of the client. This insight can then lead to subsequent changes. In the case of children, other interventions may need to be sought in order to facilitate those changes if they are found to be caused by significant others or by the child's environment.

Paul

It was believed that Paul was 8 years old and his sister about 7 when they arrived at school one wintry morning, birth certificates had not been produced; nor had previous school records. The parents seemed to speak little English, and it was difficult to communicate with them, although the Head of School seemed to think that this was an act because both children, even though they didn't talk much, understood English and did not speak another language in school. There was an understanding that they were a traveller family. Paul had been assigned to me in my role as Learning Mentor to help him adjust to the new school and to develop his confidence while further investigations were made into the family.

On the first day I met Paul, I collected him from his classroom and showed him the way to the rainbow room where I worked. It had beanbags for children to sit on, bookshelves, a crate with toys and a round table with four chairs. Immediately on entering Paul crawled under the table. No matter what I did, he didn't come out. I put a tub of crayons under the table with some pictures to colour just to see what happened, he coloured but didn't speak. When I told him that it was dinner time, he came out from under the table and I walked him back to the classroom so that he could get ready for lunch with the other children.

On the second day, Paul did the same thing: he went under the table. I wondered if he was hiding and so I played peekaboo with him. This made him laugh but he still didn't come out. On the third day, I asked his teacher how he was in class. She said that he was a strange little boy and, yes, he sometimes hid under the table.

Instead of getting better, things got worse and resignedly the teacher often gave him work to do under the table, which remarkably he did. He also still went under the table in the room we worked in but didn't play peekaboo and didn't laugh anymore. I had tried all sorts of tactics, I rolled balls to him which he rolled back if they went close to him but he wouldn't stretch to reach them. I put music on to encourage him to jump about, he was not interested. I moved the table towards the wall and ensured all the chairs were pushed tightly under when he came in but he just crawled through the legs. I put the crayons and paper a bit further away from him in hope it would entice him out. It didn't. I realised that there was something very strange in Paul hiding under the table; he would just stay there kneeling, sometimes kneeling in a squat position and sometimes on all fours. He would come out at the end when I said it was time to go back to class but I think he would have stayed there all day otherwise.

I wasn't able to see Paul every day but I did try. The children's mental health team had been contacted for advice but things were still difficult with the parents and they had moved into two other houses in the short time they had been there. The head of school didn't want to scare them away.

After probably three months including a half term week, this strange behaviour was still continuing. I had over the weeks reflected, verbally, many times, "You are under the table". "You are hiding from me". "You are on your knees under the table". This particular day I decided to get down on all fours under the table too. We stayed like that for quite a while until Paul sat back on his heels but kept his arms down with his hands on the floor. I did this too as best I could; being taller than him, my head banged on the table. All the time Paul's eyes were wide open. I didn't know if he was just surprised at me being under the table or a little bit scared but I kept eye contact for as long as I could. We stayed like this for a while longer, when, from within, I felt the overwhelming urge to bark. I held the urge for a while, thinking that it would be detrimental. However, after a moment or two, I could hold it no longer and I made a barking noise. Paul's reaction stirred me: he lifted his hands from the floor to cover his ears.

Paul:	"But I am not a dog."
Me:	"You are not a dog."
Paul:	"No, I am not a dog. Am I?" he queries.
Me:	"You are not a dog?" I query back.
	(Paul's aura completely changes. Although he does not move, I sense coldness in the atmosphere and he is deeply silent and still, his hands still over his ears)
Me:	"You are not a dog. You are under the table in the rainbow room. You have put your hands on your ears."
	(I put my hands over my ears)
Paul:	(Slowly and exaggeratedly, Paul turns his head from left to right, then up and down)

Me: *(I mirror Paul's movements and, as I do so, I am
            hit by a flashback of Paul in the school library with
            his sister. Looking along the shelves for   a book,
            they had stuck their bottoms out and had tiptoed
            along with   their arms up like floppy paws,
            laughing with their tongues out as if   they were
            panting like a dog. I can hear my heart beating;
            the feeling is intense)*
            "You are not a dog."
Paul: "No, I am not a dog. I am a boy, aren't I?" he asks.
Me: "You are not a dog. You are a boy," I reply.

I felt churned up inside. I couldn't quite comprehend what had just happened. Paul got hold of one of the cuddly toys and flopped into a bean bag. I didn't really say anything more to Paul, I sat on one of the chairs and smiled at him, got another cuddly and cuddled it. The end of session came within 5 minutes and Paul went to his class. I went into the toilet and cried.

I followed safeguarding procedure. As mentioned earlier, with some children other interventions may be needed, and this was one such case. Once Paul's case had been brought to the attention of other professionals a meeting was arranged and concerns that had been reported were shared, there were many reports of dog-like characteristics displayed by both Paul and his sister, such as Paul writing in his story, 'Daddy throws sticks for us to chase and gives us treats'. Hearing this had alarmed me because, some weeks earlier, a child from Paul's class had told me that he had brought dog biscuits for his snack at break time. At the time I had laughed because I thought they were novelty-shaped children's biscuits. I didn't go to look. Paul's sister was reported as constantly licking the back of her hands. Someone had witnessed both children sitting in assembly with their hands held up like begging dogs and Paul telling a teaching assistant "Daddy lets us chase rabbits."

Frank

Frank was 10 and the youngest sibling of a violent and dysfunctional family who tried to rule the local community. The father and mother were separated and two siblings were serving time for aggravated robbery, grievous bodily harm and manslaughter. To add to these complications, Frank had a low IQ and found schoolwork extremely difficult. His mother refused to accept this and would not sign any papers for psychological assessment or special schooling, and the Head of School was working with social services to try and find a better and safer environment for Frank. Frank's strength was that he brought himself to school because, in his words, it was "better than staying at home."

Over the previous twelve months, however, Frank had begun withdrawing from class. He expressed that the work was too difficult. His esteem had dropped to an all-time low. He felt 'thick' because he realised that lots of the younger school children could do the work that he wasn't able to do. Whereas in the past, ignoring the negative behaviour and focusing on the positive had proved somewhat successful, Frank now did not respond in a positive way to praise or encouragement. He completed only about fifteen per cent of his work and had not made any significant progress.

Frank's behaviour had changed and now he often threw items from the table on to the floor. He would hide behind the door, under the table and behind the computer and most alarming was that, when he was really stressed out, he would grab the scissors or a compass and run down the stairs, hide under them and threaten to kill himself. He was reported to have spent whole mornings in this way.

Although I had recently started counselling sessions working with Frank I had not seen any of this behaviour. However, for the class teacher things had got completely out of hand and the class was noticing that she had little control over him. One lunchtime, she approached me almost in tears to explain the difficulties she was experiencing and how she felt that she was losing him. It was agreed that I would enter class whenever it was thought that intervention might be useful.

On this particular day, Frank was squashed almost to the point of having disappeared behind the computer. I entered the classroom and wandered round looking at the other children's work, and gradually worked my way round to the computer table and Frank.

Me: "Hi Frank."
Frank: "Mmm."
Me: "Hi, Frank. I see you are squashed behind the
         computer table."
Frank: "Grrr."
Me: "Mmm, I see you are not talking."
Frank: "Grrr."
Me: "You look almost invisible squashed behind the
         computer like that."
Frank: "Grrr."
Me: "It's the middle of the morning and you are
         squashed behind the computer in your classroom.
         You look almost invisible."
Frank: "Grrr. Grrr. Grrr."
Me: "You are growling at me. I'm not sure if you want
         me to stay or go."
         (*A minute's silence*)
Me: "Mmm. You are very quiet behind the table there."
Frank: "Grrr. Grrr. Grrr."

Me: "I can see your eyes. They are peeping at me from
         under the monitor."
Frank: "GRRR. GRRR. GRRR."
Me: "You growled louder. I think you don't want me to
         see you."
Frank: (*No response*)
Me: "You look uncomfortable all squashed up behind
         there."
Frank: (*No response*)
         (*Continuing this way for around 20 minutes*)
Me: "Mmm. Now you have stopped growling at me. It
         is morning and you are squashed up behind the
         computer. You have been here quite a while. You
         came here during literacy hour and now it is
         numeracy hour. All the other boys and girls have
         changed tables."
Frank: (*No response*)
Me: "You know what? I'm wondering if there is room
         for two behind there."
         (*I squash myself behind the computer table so that
         I am side by side with Frank*)
         "My! This is a tight squeeze. Now I am behind the
         computer table with you."
Frank: (*No response*)
Me: "It feels warm behind here and I see you can rest
         your bottom on that little piece of shelf unit."
Frank: (*No response*)
Me: "I'm wondering how you feel tucked up behind
         here."
Frank: (*No response*)
Me: "Mmm, now I can see you look quite comfortable
         sitting here on Tuesday morning during numeracy
         hour."

Frank: (*No response*)
Me: "We have been here a long time now. It is Tuesday
          and we are in your classroom. The other children
          are doing literacy. It seems you don't want to do
          numeracy. It seems you just want to stay here,
          behind the computer, peeping through the little
          gap."
Frank: (*Shuffles his feet, turns his head to face me and
          smiles*)
          "Nobody can see me."
Me: "Nobody can see you."
Frank: "I can see everybody."
Me: "You can see everybody."
Frank: "I like seeing everybody."
Me: "You like seeing everybody."
Frank: "I like nobody seeing me."
Me: "You like nobody seeing you."
Frank: "I have a spy hole and they don't know I am
          watching them."
Me: "You have a spy hole to watch them through. You
          like seeing them but you don't like them seeing
          you."
Frank: "Move now. I want to get out."
          (*We both clamber out from behind the computer
          table*)

I spent more times like this with Frank; it became a successful way
of working at the heart of the problem: lying on the floor in the
corridor looking under the crack at the bottom of the door; hiding
behind the door in the PE corridor. Necessary changes were made;
one being that Frank chose to sit at a table at the back of the
classroom where he could be separate from the other children, but
also there was a space for him to join in if he wished. At the final

review before I finished working at the school, it was realised that Frank had not retreated under the stairs or threatened to kill himself for quite a few months.

Obviously, and sadly, intervention in childhood is not always possible. Therefore, any mental health problems will be carried forward into adulthood.

Losing inhibitions and self-consciousness has been one of the greatest advances to the success of Pre-Therapy within my practice and working in an environment where other people are not trained and do not understand counselling or Pre-Therapy is where, at first, I had to overcome my embarrassment. It must seem pretty odd to the onlooker to see a grown adult lying on the floor looking through a crack under the door or sitting under a table. I know that I would look twice.

Shirley

Shirley in her late 20's self-referred for counselling through a local charity. She had been advised to get some counselling by her boss, who told her that she did strange things sometimes. Shirley had no memory of strange things and didn't elaborate on what her boss said that she did.

The room we used was in a nursing home office and had a large desk, which was pushed to the end of the room, and there were two executive swivel chairs. We had worked together for a few months, exploring what she termed as 'a strange life'. Educated at a girl's boarding school, where she was bullied and sexually abused by other girls, leading her to be confused about her sexuality, this had led her to move away from her wealthy parents into an abusive relationship. In therapy, she had examined and overcome some very obsessive and self-destructive behaviour. Shirley had cried, banged, shouted, felt despair and loneliness, and all these had been shared in the therapy, yet there were still some years that Shirley could not recall; some years she had lost.

Fidgeting continually, crossing and uncrossing her legs and spinning around on the chair, Shirley would talk fast, looking around the room but not making eye contact. Whereas Psychological Contact had been constant, it was now patchy. It seemed to me that, every time Shirley got closer to an unexpressed feeling, her whole demeanour changed: before my eyes she seemed to shrink – disappear almost – becoming very still and silent.

Puzzled, this change in the therapeutic relationship concerned me. Endeavouring to regain contact, I tried a variety of different ways to communicate but, because Shirley didn't respond, I was lost. Sometimes, I just sat there, not really knowing what to say or do. I felt that we became separated. I talked in supervision about Shirley, about my sense of missing something important even though Shirley had explored a great deal. My supervisor suggested not just listening but to observe much more closely Shirley's body language or facial expressions.

We were perhaps in our nineteenth session when I noticed that Shirley, in the quietness where we lost contact with each other, lifted her feet off the floor by an inch or two and held her knees with her hands.

I very slowly lifted my feet off the floor too and, as I did so, Shirley lifted hers higher until her feet were on the chair and her arms were wrapped around her knees. I mirrored her as best I could, resting my feet on the chair too, and we sat in this position for around five minutes. At this moment, I felt a shift: my attitude changed, my empathy overwhelmed me and I felt a connection with my client. Working spontaneously in the very moment enabled Shirley to receive my empathy and we again became one. Shirley had her head turned away from me but moved her eyes to meet mine. She spoke very slowly and clearly.

Shirley "Nobody has been on my branch before."

Me   "Nobody has been on your branch before."
Shirley   Yes. You are the first person. I thought it might
          break.
Me   "I am the first person to sit on your branch and you
          thought it would break if I sat on it."
Shirley   "We are both on the branch now."

We sat in this position for about five minutes; neither of us speaking. It wasn't necessary because the atmosphere around us became warm and I felt Shirley begin to relax. She continued to look over at me, carefully watching my body, checking my face and eyes. Slowly, her shoulders became less rigid, even though she kept her arms wrapped around her knees and her feet on the chair. We were experiencing very deep Psychological Contact; it was precise and detailed. I knew she felt it too. I felt an overwhelming urge to cry. Shirley put her hands to her head and lowered her feet to the ground. She leant over, keeping her hands over her face, and rested her elbows on her knees. I put my feet on the ground and, as I did so, Shirley sat up and looked at me. There was a slow, precise abnormality about the way in which she spoke.

Shirley: "I have always sat on my branch. I can lift my feet
          right up and I am completely hidden by the tree.
          That way, no one can see me. Nobody can see me
          from above or below and all sides of me are well
          hidden."
Me: "When you sit on your branch you are completely
          hidden by the tree. Nobody can see you then."
Shirley: "Mmm, nobody."
Me: "Nobody."
Shirley: "Mmm, safe. Hidden in my tree."
Me: "Safe. Hidden in your tree."

Shirley: "Oh yes. It has always been important, but now I realise that other people can climb the tree if they want."

Me: "Others can climb the tree now."

(*There is a few minutes' pause where I feel myself losing contact with Shirley again. I watch her closely for tiny movements, when I see her slowly lifting her feet slightly and then putting them back down again.*

The same distancing seems to be happening again)

Me: "It feels safe in the tree. Nobody can see you."

Shirley: (*Still far away*)

Me: "But people can climb the tree if they want." (*I raise my feet and rest them on the chair, with my arms wrapped around my knees; mirroring Shirley's earlier actions*)

(*Slowly Shirley turns to look at me, her eyes still glazed and speaking very slowly and precisely*)

Shirley: "The wind and rain come out of my head."

Me: "The wind and rain come out of my head." (*I place my feet back on the floor, pause for about a minute, during which time I again feel an overwhelming urge to cry*)

Me: "It feels very sad that the wind and rain come out of your head."

Shirley: (*Nods. A tear rolls down her cheek*)

Me: "I see you cry."

Shirley: "It is very sad. It is very sad."

(*Shirley becomes aware of the room again, then of me. Her eyes lose their glaze and her body posture softens. She begins to swivel on the chair again. I feel that we are 'back'; grounded*)

Shirley: "I think I have been very ill. Do you think I've
been very ill? I have been very ill."
(*Pause*)
"I lived up that tree for a very long time."
Me: "I hear you."
Shirley: "I was a hermit, a recluse. Didn't speak to anyone,
took milk off doorsteps, ate out of bins. Was it
really me? I thought I was in control of the
weather. I really thought I was living in a tree but
of course I wasn't. Where have I been?"
Me: "It seems so confusing right now. There is so
much…"
Shirley: "How will I manage without my tree?"
Me: "…like, without your tree you will have to find
another way of coping."
Shirley: "How did it all happen?"
Me: "So many questions are coming to you right now.
How did it happen? How will you manage?"
Shirley: "Mmm. I feel exhausted. I feel really strange. I am
not sure what is real anymore."

Shirley finished therapy four sessions after this, saying she just needed time now to think, to accept how ill she had been and to work out what her choices in life were. Our last session was very emotional:

"I am going to miss my tree. It's been a good way of coping but I know the branches are full of shit and one by one I am going to look at them. But not now.

When you came up the tree with me it was a wonderful moment. Suddenly everything I wanted to say didn't need to be said. All my life, up the tree at different times, it kept me sort of safe, but I know now that my mother could have tried to get in the tree with me but she never tried." (Gentle *cry*) "If my mother had been a mother I wouldn't have needed the tree. It might have kept me safe, but it was lonely, cold, wet and frightening. One move and I would have fallen, dead. That's how it felt. That's how I felt most of my life. That's how it felt with you at first; cold and not really real." (*Deep sigh*) "I felt nobody in the world could reach me. Well, they couldn't, could they? I took myself away from everybody in my mind.

When I have been up my tree, I wonder what I looked like to other people. I thought they really couldn't see me, but you showed me that I can't be invisible; tree or no tree."

Never having been for counselling before, and never having any mental health diagnosis, Shirley had somehow survived; her actualising tendency striving forward had now led her to new and safe conditions in which to grow. Reaching this point was aided by Pre-Therapy, where Shirley discovered and began to look at the reality which had caused her to take herself away in her mind.

I found this to be an encouraging and emotional ending, confirming that powerful beyond all measure is a person's drive and ability to get well.

Personal Experience

I could tell that my counsellor was trying to be with me but I also knew that I had moved to a very strange and scary place. For two or three sessions this continued. After a session I found it very difficult to get back in touch with reality, to drive the car or to make a meal. I seemed to have split into two. I also felt on the borderline for 'my people' returning. Indeed, I saw fragments of them. One morning, I woke to see Mikey (hallucination) sitting on the chair in the bedroom. This too was frightening. I began to get very strong suicidal feelings, which I didn't want to share with my counsellor, due to bad experiences from the past where I had been sectioned. It was a very scary, strange situation; I didn't know how to change it. I was terrified at this point of falling backwards. I was very aware of how fine a line I was treading.

Prior to the next session, I had thought to stop the therapy because it seemed too dangerous and I couldn't see us breaking through. I sat in the chair again – the same goddamn chair! My strength went almost immediately and, again, I was fighting images. I remember wanting to hold my hand out to my counsellor and show him the sperm that had squirted on my hand. I wanted to say how sick I felt. I knew my counsellor had no idea what I was seeing or thinking, and there was no way I could tell him. I remember silently urging him to read my mind but he didn't hear me. I was paralysed and we were miles apart. Slowly, my counsellor reflected to me how I was sitting; he reflected that I looked like a terrified child curled up in the foetal position. I remember then being able to look at him as he too took up the same position.

I knew then I didn't need to explain anything. I felt as though he had joined me, and I suddenly saw how I looked. I felt like a very vulnerable young person. I was overwhelmed by many different emotions all at once. Then I smiled. I felt the tension leave my body. The huge black void that I had been treading around the edges of in earlier sessions suddenly swept over me and I realised that I was holding the small delicate child that was myself very tightly so that I wouldn't get lost. This was a very powerful moment.

I left the session quite shaken up, drained, tired, but a little freer. I took a stroll down to the beach. As I was walking along it, carrying myself, the younger me, something wonderful happened. Just like clicking your fingers – it was that sudden – I knew. I knew that it wasn't my fault. I felt as though it wasn't my fault. It felt as though a whirlpool had opened up around me and I was swirling around inside it, freeing myself of guilt, exploding with anger at the bastard who rightly deserved it. Something big had shifted. I ran, I cried, I laughed. I span round and round. I swore, I screamed and I shouted. I was wild like the wind but, more than that, much more than that, I was free.

During the week that followed, I had mood swings and often cried huge, exploding sobs or completely shook with laughter. I acknowledged that the abuse had not been my fault; none of it. Neither what he did to me nor what he did to the other children. It wasn't my fault. I couldn't even work out why I thought it had been, in fact I don't think I was consciously aware that I thought it was my fault. At the next session, I was comfortably able to end my counselling; I was back to where I needed to be. Sensing that a change had begun after he had used body, situation and facial reflections, but having no idea what was going on for me, my counsellor told me, "I didn't strive to understand at that point; I only strove to regain contact." That to me speaks of Pre-Therapy.

The reader can gain encouragement from the above scenario, maybe accessing some training, talking over in supervision and with colleagues will help Pre-Therapy become integrated as part therapeutic practice.

During the early stages of development using Pre-Therapy could prevented serious mental health issues developing because the pre-expressive will become expressed and therefore the difficulties will not become manifest. In other cases where safeguarding issues are raised, interventions will be put in place by other services which will prevent further harm and so evert the development of further mental distress.

Throughout all the above scenarios the decision to use, and the flexibility of, Pre-Therapy reflections had a positive effect on the therapeutic relationship, on the facilitation of Psychological Contact and on the movement of therapeutic change. These reflections do not always flow easily and the reader could agree with Pietrzac (1994) "the techniques are simple but the practice is difficult." However, having said that, once started and integrated, the process does become easier.

CHAPTER 7:

INVOLUNTARY CLIENTS

In the field of counselling and psychotherapy it is often said that the client has to be ready for therapy or there will be no significant therapeutic process. Even if other people suggest it to the individual or say it will help, only when the person is ready and able to engage will therapy begin.

Looking closer on this point it seems that key elements from Rogers' hypothesised "necessary conditions for a therapeutic relationship" (1961) are missing in the involuntary relationship. By looking at the "Seven Stages of Process to Personality Change" (1951) and "A theory of personality and behaviour" (1951), this chapter will discover the missing elements while also exploring the use of Pre-Therapy as a key to success in this area.

Rogers "Theory of Personality and behaviour" (1951), which has 19 stages, is the proposed journey a person takes to become fully functioning. There is much more writing on what is meant by fully functioning by many authors and Rogers himself, this is widely available on-line and from book stores.

To generalise a fully functioning person would live in the here and now of life and be able to reflect on their opinions, feelings and behaviours. Such a person would be in tune with their deepest emotions, intimate thoughts and wildest dreams. Being true to their self. When challenged on their self-concept a person who is fully functioning will be able to reflect and explore the new aspect and if they decide to they can accept this new concept as part of themselves.

Theory of personality and behaviour. Proposition 11

As experiences occur in the life of the individual, they are:

    a) Symbolised, perceived and organised into some relationship to the self.

    b) Ignored because there is no perceived relationship to the self-structure.

    c) Denied symbolisation or given a distorted symbolisation because the experience is inconsistent with the structure of self.

Looking at the proposition above the reader can recognise that 11b and 11c would probably best describe the process that a person who does not think they 'need' counselling

The seven stages of process to personality change.

The Seven Stages of Process to Personality Change' (Rogers, 1951) refers to the flexible back and forth movement a person goes through whilst trying to make personal change. The stages range from 1, a rigid self-belief with "remoteness from experiencing" to 7 "experiencing effective choices of new ways of being" (Feltham and Dryden 1993). These are stages a person will go through once they start exploring their experiences and feeling in a counselling relationship.

Stage 1.

- The individual at this stage of rigidity and remoteness of experiencing is not likely to come voluntarily to therapy.
- No problems are recognised or perceived. There is no wish to change. Close relationships seem dangerous.
- The individual is not in touch with their feelings and also relate all present experiences to past experiences, and reacts to the past experience; not to the here and now experience.

Stage 2

- Experiencing may begin to flow in regard to non-self topics.
- Any problems are external to self. Locus of evaluation will be external. There will be a sense of helplessness, no sense that they have the ability to do something about situations. No sense of personal responsibility.
- The client may touch on a feeling but will not own it, so they may say about a situation, "It was the anger that made me…", rather than "I felt so angry I…"
- Personal constructs are thought of as facts: "This is the way it is or I am."
- "I never get anything right." "I can't do anything properly." "I always ruin everything."

Considering the above information therefore leads to an understanding that an involuntary client will:

- Have been 'sent' for counselling or has arrived through the suggestion of others.
- See no direct connection between one's self, behaviour and problems.
- Perceive everybody else as having the problem.
- Ignore, deny or distort experiences.

Therefore, an involuntary client would suffer no incongruence.

- Lack of incongruence in the client, does not meet Roger's second hypothesised 'necessary requirements for a therapeutic relationship' (Rogers, 1951). "The first, whom we shall term the client, is in a state of incongruence, being vulnerable or anxious."

Roger's first hypothesised condition "Two persons are in Psychological Contact." is also missing.
- Therefore, no therapeutic relationship is formed.

Confirming "A person does not become a client until he or she decides to become one." (Patterson)

Consider the idea that Pre-Therapy can be used as a tool to lead a person to their incongruence safely while also facilitating Psychological Contact.

Sophie

Within the school environment, the role of counsellor also included being part of the 'rapid response' team, which operated a rota system to manage any behavioural issues that came up during the course of the day. Fourteen-year-old Sophie was 'sent' for counselling and, even though she didn't really want to, she turned up for sessions once a week for one hour, "Cos it's better than class and I'd get done if I don't come."

Sophie, according to her significant others, often bullied, threatened, swore, kicked and thumped others, seemingly without provocation. Any praise given was rebuffed, any criticism was exaggerated out of proportion and it seemed that Sophie had no trust in anyone.

One bright sunny morning, Sophie marched into classroom, viciously kicked another girl of the same age on her leg, grabbed her hair, pushing the girl's head on to the wall, kicked her again, then tried to walk away, whereby in retaliation, she was pulled back and a brawl began. After separating the two, Sophie was isolated and given space and time to calm down. After this time, I entered the time-out room.

Key
P: Proposition
S: Stage

Sophie	"I never did anything." (P. 11. Denial.) (*Sitting on a chair by the window*)
Me	"Mmm. You didn't do anything." (*Sitting on a chair near the client*)
Sophie	"Yeah, right. I didn't do anything." (*I move my chair away from the window and sit on it*)
Me	"Mmm, I hear you." (*I turn my chair round*)
Sophie	(*Shaking her head and banging the back of the chair*) "I didn't. It were an accident." (P.11 Distortion) "I don't kick." (P.11 Ignored) "I was tryin' to kick the chair. Anyway, it was her fault." (S.2. No ownership) (*I stand up, push the chair away and walk back to the window*)
Me	"Mmm, so it was all her fault. I hear you. It wasn't your fault; you were trying to kick the chair. I can see that you are still feeling angry and upset; maybe worried because you are in trouble with staff."

(*I stay sitting and turn my chair to face her again*)

    Sophie"I'm not fuckin angry!" (P.11 Denial)
"I don't do fuckin' angry!" (*making inverted comma sign with her hands*)
"You silly fuckin' cow! She just pissed me off. Okay?"
(S.2. No ownership of feeling)
(*Sophie walks over to a chair, kicks it and then pulls it over backwards*)
    "Get it?"

Me	"I get it. She just pissed you off. So you feel pissed off."
Sophie	"You moron! No. I don't feel fuckin' pissed of now! She pissed me off. Right? But I don't feel nothing. Understand? (Sophie walks back towards the window then changes direction and sits on a table top.
Me	"Mmm, sounds really hard. You feel nothing. Right?"
Sophie:	"I didn't do nothing wrong. She always gets me into trouble! She makes me do stuff an' I get into trouble for it. It's her fault, stupid effin bitch! Next time she gets me in trouble I'll swing for her. It's all her stinkin' fault!" (S.1)

Evident at this stage of development, Sophie has a high external locus of evaluation, blaming others for her behaviour and her feelings. Not only does Sophie 'not do' angry, she doesn't do sad, upset, frightened, worried or a whole range of other emotions and feelings. Sophie has no wish to change. Why should she? In her eyes, she doesn't have a problem; she is experiencing no incongruence. Sophie is clearly an involuntary client within Stage 1 of the process of personality change.

During Sophie's next counselling session, she did not refer to the incident; nor did I. Remarkably, neither did she refer to even one of her own feelings, although she was able to tell me how someone else felt. Although Sophie attended the session, we made no significant progress, not even on building trust, because, as she clearly explained, "You belong to the school, get paid to do the job and that is the only reason you're here. It's not like you're really bothered."

I decided to use the Pre-Therapy strategies with Sophie, because, at the end of the day, I felt that I was fighting a losing battle. Every session seemed to become a battleground. If I reflected a felt sense, she denied it or spat it back at me. If I reflected a mood, she became angry and would bang or slam something or even throw something. When I showed empathy, she thought I was patronising and reacted accordingly. I felt worlds apart from Sophie; we were not in Psychological Contact so there was no therapeutic relationship. I felt I needed to facilitate Psychological Contact and decided on using Pre-Therapy as a strategy to help me reach her.

It was about four days later when I first put Pre-Therapy into action. Sophie had kicked one of the other girls and had pushed her against a wall, threatening to "smash her tiny little brain in." One of the members of staff had forcefully pulled her away and, with assistance, had moved her to the time-out room, where Sophie had kicked the table over and thrown two chairs against the wall, while using much explicit language and name calling. Now seeing that everything was much calmer I went inside.

On seeing me, Sophie threw herself on to the table, crossed one leg one over the other, folded her arms and turned her head away from me. I took up the same position on the other side of the table; the only difference being that my head was facing hers, but I held the same facial expression. The strange thing is, when I sat exactly the same way, I became hugely aware of how defensive she was feeling. Taking up her body position put me straight into her frame of reference.

Sophie 1	"Yeah, what the fuck you doin'?"
Me 1	"You are sitting on the table, in the time-out room, arms folded, legs crossed and ask me, 'Yea what the fuck you doin'"?
Sophie 2	"Yeah, well I don't look like that, you geek."
Me 2	"I hear you. 'Yeah, well I don't look like that, you geek'."
Sophie 3	*"Aren't you supposed to be havin' 'a nice quiet little word' with me?"*
Me 3	*"You asked, aren't I supposed to be havin' 'a nice quiet little word' with me?"* *(I maintain the same body position as she does)*
Sophie 4	*(Gets off the table and walks over towards the window. She stands looking outside)* *"I didn't do nothin'."*
Me 4	*"You didn't do nothin'. And you are looking out of the window."*
Sophie 5	*"Yeah, I know what I've done. I ain't stupid."* *(She turns around and stares at me, with anger burning in her eyes)*
Me 5	*(I move slightly to sit on the edge of the table)* *"You are staring at me. You look angry. Your body is very tense."*
Sophie 6	"What is this? Some kind of new fuckin' 'therapy'? Don't think you can break me down." *(She looks out of the window)* "I am unbreakable."

(*She folds her arms, leans back on the window ledge and stares right into my*
"I didn't do nothin'. You're supposed to be getting me to say I've done somethin' that I aint!"

Me 6 "You feel I'm trying to get you to say you have done something you haven't." (*I fold my arms and stay sitting on the end of the table*) "You said, 'I am unbreakable. Don't think you can break me down'. And you're staring right into my eyes."

Sophie 7 "Yeah, well I am unbreakable. Many have tried and many have failed. Don't think you are any different from the rest." (*Sophie's stare relaxes and she looks down at her feet*)

Me 7 "You're looking down at your feet and you tell me you are unbreakable. Telling me many have tried and many have failed."

Sophie 8 "Why the fuck does the whole bloody world have to try and fuckin' destroy me? Why the fuck does every Goddamn person hate me, and why the fuck can't I just get some fuckin' peace?
(*She kicks the wall, moves to the corner of the room and slides to the floor*) "Everybody just thinks they know better."

Me 8 (*I go and sit opposite Sophie and take up her body position*).
"I hear you. 'Why the fuck can't you just get some fuckin' peace?' You look very sad."

Sophie 9 (*Covers her face with her hands*)

Me 9 "I notice you have covered your face."

Sophie 10   "Please, Miss, just stop now. If I cry I won't
             stop."
Me 10   "It's okay to cry."
Sophie 11   (*Crying*)

This was a turning point in therapy. In fact, this was the beginning of therapeutic change. Sophie had let down her guard and shown her vulnerability. This would not have happened if it were not for the Pre-Therapy reflections.

I feel that, in this instance, Sophie saw and heard herself probably for the first time. I feel that, by mirroring her body language, she saw her own behaviour and, on hearing the WWR, she also heard her own words, and this had an impact on her.

I was very aware of Sophie feeling vulnerable and defensive at Sophie 6 and at Me 6. Offering her the WWR, I kept my voice level and ensured no patronisation. I feel that this was significant. Neither did I strive to reassure, which, from past experience, she could have perceived as a trick or an attempt to 'break' her.

Under no threat to be broken, I feel that Sophie's demeanour began to change at Sophie 7, when she released her stare and looked down at her feet. I felt that this showed some kind of inward reflection and maybe touched on her incongruence, which is confirmed in Sophie 8, where she verbalises her vulnerability and hurt.

Interestingly, in Me 8, at the point where I turned the reflections from exact WWR and exchanged the use of 'I' to 'you', Sophie received my empathy, which is why she was able to cry. I feel that this was an intense moment of Psychological Contact.

Certainly, Sophie's tears moved me. I had not envisaged this. I know that the she too was surprised at her own vulnerability and the fact that she started crying, because after the session she begged me to swear, "Not to tell another living soul."

I feel that there was a risk involved and that Sophie could have thought that I was mimicking her, and this could have been a source of her anger. However, she did not react in that way, thereby enabling the success of the Pre-Therapy reflections.

Seriously aggressive behaviour, leading to a series of exclusions from school and a warning of permanent exclusion, John at age 15 sees no problem with the way in which he behaves, and feels that he is not aggressive, even after head-butting another pupil, who needed four stitches in his forehead. Consequently, John was told to attend counselling with me, whereby, after six weeks, I had made no headway with him. He had not turned up for any sessions and ignored any coaxing and prompting. During the seventh week, I unexpectedly came across him after he'd been sent out of class for bad behaviour. He was sitting on the stairs, head in hands and was staring through his fingers. I sat down next to him and, when he made no response to my presence, I spoke to him.

Me	You're just sitting on the stairs with your head in your hands staring at your feet." (*I sit with him for 2 or 3 minutes*)
John	(*Moves his hands and looks out of the window*)
Me:	"Now you are looking out of the window." (*I want to make eye contact, so I move parallel to him on the stairs, so that the window is behind me. I look at John, but he doesn't move or make eye contact*

The bell rang for period changeover. I explained to John that I needed to go because I was meeting with other pupils. I stood up to go and, just out of the corner of my eye, I saw him look at me. It didn't occur to me to stay with him longer, nor do I have any idea what he did next. Did he stay in the corridor or did he go to his next class?

At the time of our next session, when John did not turn up I was disappointed. I thought he might have come. I decided to go and find him. This change came about through thinking of Pre-Therapy and that it is the therapist's role to make the move to 'be with' the client because the client may be unable to come to the therapist.

This was quite a change from my previous learning, where I had been taught not to go running after children because it fed their need for attention and encouraged them to 'keep on running'. Now I was re-learning. John certainly wasn't seeking my attention. I felt I had nothing to lose. After all, so far, I had got nowhere.

Surprisingly, John was only on the floor above my room, leaning over the banister. I spoke but he didn't respond.

Me	(*I take up the same position as him and reflect to him what he is doing*) (BR)
John	(*John's face holds no expression; we stay like this for around 10 minutes. Then suddenly he pushes himself off the banister and sits on the floor with his back against the wall*)
Me:	(*I sit against the banister facing John and mirror his body position*) "You're sitting in the school corridor, leaning against the wall, staring straight ahead.
John	(*After a few minutes, John slowly lifts his head, looks at me and shakes his head*)(*I too shake my head*) (BR) (*At this moment, I feel something change; just slightly. We maintain eye contact for around 3 seconds*)
John:	(*Turns away for a moment then stands up and looks at me*) "It's not just that.
Me:	(*Standing up*) (BR) "It's not just that." (WWR)

John   (*John looks at me for a few seconds, sighs and
            walks off*)

On reflection, I could have gone with John, but at the time it didn't occur to me to do so. Beaten, I went back to my room. 'It's not just what?' I wondered. However, for the time being I was aware that I did not need to understand; I needed to concentrate on gaining contact. There were still twenty minutes to go before period end. About three minutes before the bell went, John entered my room and sat on the chair.

John   (*Puts his head in his hands and stares at his feet*)
Me   "You've come in the room and now you are sitting
            in the chair. Your bag is on the floor and you are
            looking at your feet." (SR/BR)
John   Remains looking down
Me   "It's not just that." (RR)
John   (*No response*)
            (*The school bell sounds. John picks up his bag,
            walks to the door, turns around, looks at me and
            leaves*)

Marking a huge milestone, John appeared on time for his next appointment. Placing his bag on the floor and sitting in a chair he looked me in the eye, leant back and said, "Can I choose what we do?"

Reflecting on the process, our therapeutic work began with the use of Pre-Therapy, when I went to, and stayed with, John. I had a direction and a purpose: to facilitate Psychological Contact with John, build up his trust in me and somehow get him to come to my room regularly. It worked. I feel that this worked because I entered into John's world; just to be with him as he was. Everything I offered was unconditional; everything I showed him and said to him was a mirror of his self.

A whole array of disruptive and withdrawn behaviours could be accredited to Carl, who would deny them all. Staff reported that he had 'gone off on one' some twenty minutes earlier; nobody seeming sure of the reason, nor sure of his destination. Finding Carl sitting on the floor in the boys' toilets, I entered

Me	"Hi Carl. I've just come to see if you are okay."
Carl	(*No response*).
Me	(*I sit on the floor facing him*)
Carl	(*No response*) (*30 seconds later*)
Me	"Carl, you are sitting on the floor in the boys' toilets."
Carl	(*No response*)

(*30 seconds later*)

Me	"Carl, you have your head in your hands and you are staring down at your knees." (*I change my position here to be more like his, because I become aware that Carl can probably see me from between his arms*)
Carl	(*No response*)

(*30 seconds later*)

Me	"Carl, it is a Friday afternoon and you are sitting on the floor in the boys' toilets…"
Carl	(*Suddenly jumps up*) "Stop mimicking me and takin' the piss!" (*Walks out of the toilets and into the craft room where he begins talking to another member of staff*)

I was very surprised at this reaction because I expected to be in the toilets with Carl for at least another twenty minutes, and the suddenness of him getting up and leaving the room left me somewhat stunned. Although Carl did get back in touch with the shared reality, I sense that he felt threatened, rather than accepted. I also sense that he felt that I was challenging him, rather than offering him unconditional positive regard. My thoughts are, what would have happened if Carl had come back to the shared reality at a point of intense anger and his reaction had been a violent one? Was I unprepared and was my safety at risk?

When talking about this with a colleague, we couldn't quite decide whether the therapy was relevant or successful. After some deliberations we found the following points significant.

- Carl could have stayed on the floor in the toilets for quite a lot longer; he has been known to stay that way for an entire afternoon.
- The aim of the therapy was to bring Carl back into contact with the shared reality, which it did.
- Thirdly, Carl did enter into a congruent relationship with the member of staff in the craft room.

The reader may find that considering the use of Pre-Therapy reflections with involuntary clients' needs more attention as a theory, yet, it may seem relevant to pursue. Good use of supervision and preparation for outbursts and unpredictable behaviour must be made to ensure the safety of those concerned. Once these precautionary measures are in place, Pre-Therapy can indeed be used successfully with involuntary clients, both to lead to awareness of incongruence and as a facilitator towards Psychological Contact.

<u>CONCLUSION</u>

Throughout this book the reader has journeyed through the history of Pre-Therapy so as to understand the origins. Learning the importance and value of psychological contact and what it means to both therapist and client and also how it feels for both when it is not there. The reader has been assisted with step by step guide and explanation of Contact Reflections, Functions and Behaviours to understand the strength of these in enabling entry into the personal world of the other.

Throughout the journey extracts from client work has been shared and explored to give a theoretical understanding of the process that takes place. These scenarios are both from clinical therapeutic practice and other situations which people who are not counsellors or psychotherapists, may come across in their day to day life.

Over the years of developing this book many people as well as therapists have given me an insight into their own experiences of using Pre-therapy. A mother gave me an example of how it helped her to make bath times easier for her son with learning difficulties. A nurse told how it has helped settle patients. A psychiatric nurse has used the techniques many times as an aid to calming patients in psychosis and he has gone on to introduce the techniques to his colleagues. Two geriatric nurses have given feedback that these strategies can be useful in gaining contact with people displaying the onset of dementia and a police officer said it has helped prevent antagonistic behaviour during arrests and questioning.

It is on a therapeutic level though that I find passion. One question that Van Werde asked when emailed regarding some work done with a child, maybe a couple of years before this book was finished, was, 'Why do you want to bring the client back to the shared reality?' I didn't respond because I didn't at the time know the answer. I feel now that I can answer and it is in two parts. First it is not that I want to bring the client back to the shared reality but more I aim to create a therapeutic space, where the client becomes aware of their reality and can share it with me, where I can then join their reality and show an empathic understanding. The client's reality shared. Then secondly it would be that the clients I work with function on a daily basis in the realms of normal functioning and social interaction so I feel it would be unethical to leave the client in any other way than in the shared reality.

On this point, there have been occasions where other support has been sought because the client has become too distressed and unable to manage their daily life or been at risk to their self or others. This can happen without the use of Pre-Therapy too.

I had the privilege of speaking via email to Garry Prouty, once in 2006 and again in 2008, on both occasions he offered his encouragement as I am offering you, to use the theory of psychological contact named Pre-therapy in any therapeutic way in which it could aid in easing the unnecessary mental suffering of another person

REFERENCES

Feltham C & Dryden W (1993) Dictionary of Counselling, London. Whurr (cited on Counsellingtutor.com
Mearns, D. 1996. Working at relational depth with clients in person centred therapy. Paper. Glasgow.   University of Strathclyde.
Mearns and Thorne. 1999. Person centred counselling in action. London. Sage.
Mearns, D. 2007. Person Centred Counselling Training. Sage. London.
Prouty, Van Werde, Portner. 1994. Pre-Therapy. Ross on Wyre. PCCS Books.
Prouty, G. 1990. Theoretical Evaluations in person centred / Experiential Therapy. Greenwood Press.
Prouty, G. 2002. Contact and Perception. 2002.
Roger, C.R. 1951. Client Centred Therapy. Constable. London.
Rogers, C. R. 1957. The necessary and sufficient conditions of therapeutic personality change. Journal of Consulting Psychology. University of Chicago.
Rogers, C. R. 1980. A way of being. Boston Houghton Mifflin.
Sommerbeck, L. 2006. Beyond Psychotherapeutic Reach. Paper. WAPCEP Website.
Sanders, P. 2007.The contact work primer. PCCS.
The Focusing Institute Gendlin Online Library.

BIBLIOGRAPHY

Bozarth, J. and Tamaner Brodley, B. 1986. The core values and Theory of the person - centred approach. Paper. Chicago.
Brazier, D. 1993. Beyond Carl Rogers. London. Constable.

Brazier, D. & Beech, C. Empathy for a real world. Paper. Newcastle.

Feltham C & Dryden W (1993) Dictionary of Counselling, London. Whurr (cited on Counsellingtutor.com

Hogan, R. 1948. The development of a measure of client defensiveness in the counselling relationship. Ph.D. Thesis abstract, University of Chicago.

Kirschenbaun and Henderson. 1990. The Carl Rogers reader. London. Constable.

Lipton, B. H. 2005. The Biology of Belief. California. Hay House.

Mearns, D. 1996. Working at relational depth with clients in person centred therapy. Paper. University of Strathclyde. Glasgow.

Mearns and Thorne. 1999. Person centred counselling in action. London. Sage.

Mearns, D. 2007. Person Centred Counselling Training. London. Sage.

Merry, T. 1999. Learning and being in person centred counselling. Ross on Wye. PCCS Books.

Merry, T. 2000.   Person Centred Psychotherapy. London. Sage.

Moon, J. A. 2004. A handbook of Reflective and Experiential Learning. London and New York.

Pearsall, J. 2011. The Concise Oxford Dictionary. Oxford. University Press. Routledge Falmer.

Prouty, Van Werde, Portner. 1994. Pre-Therapy. Ross on Wyre. PCCS Books.

Prouty, G. 1990. Theoretical Evaluations in person centred / Experiential Therapy. Greenwood Press.

Prouty, G. 2002. Contact and Perception. Ross on Wyre. PCCS Books.

Rogers, C. R. 1951. Client Centred Therapy. London. Constable.

Rogers, C. R. 1957. The necessary and sufficient conditions of therapeutic personality change. The journal of consulting psychology. . University of Chicago.
Rogers, C. R. 1961. On becoming a Person. London. Constable.
Rogers, C. R. 1980. A way of being. Boston Houghton Mifflin.
Sommerbeck, L. 2006. Beyond Psychotherapeutic Reach. Paper. WAPCEP Website. Sanders, P. 2007.The contact work primer. Ross on Wyre. PCCS Books.